ISRAEL'S MISSION TO THE WORLD

BY

H. H. ROWLEY, M.A., B.Litt., D.D.

PROFESSOR OF SEMITIC LANGUAGES,
UNIVERSITY COLLEGE, BANGOR

LONDON
STUDENT CHRISTIAN MOVEMENT PRESS
58 BLOOMSBURY STREET, W.C.1

TO

THE REVEREND PREBENDARY

W. O. E. OESTERLEY

D.D., Litt.D.

SCHOLAR AND FRIEND,
THIS VOLUME IS INSCRIBED
IN GRATITUDE AND ESTEEM

First Published in February 1939

PRINTED IN GREAT BRITAIN BY
MORRISON AND GIBB LTD., LONDON AND EDINBURGH

PREFACE

THE four chapters of this book were delivered as lectures to the Vacation Term for Biblical Study in Oxford in August 1938, and are published at the request of some of those to whom they were delivered, who believed they might be more widely useful in this form to those who are charged with the task of teaching the Old Testament. I should have preferred to expand the lectures before publishing them, and to have offered some discussion of many points, instead of bare statement. The pressure of other work made this impossible at the moment, however, and the result would probably have been a work of less general usefulness. I have therefore published them with only very minor changes, in the hope that, despite the slightness of treatment imposed by the limits of four lectures, these studies may contribute to a juster estimate of our debt to Israel than is generally recognised to-day.

I wish to record my warm thanks to Mr. Herbert Loewe, M.A., of Cambridge, for his kindness in reading through my manuscript, and for a number of valuable suggestions ; to Miss E. W. Hippisley, S.Th., without whose initiative these studies would not have been published; and to Dr. Basil Yeaxlee, Editor of *Religion in Education*, for his permission to reproduce the fourth chapter, which has already appeared in that journal in a slightly abridged form.

H. H. ROWLEY.

CONTENTS

CHAPTER I

THE WIDER VISION

THE older view of the Old Testament, which attributed the entire Pentateuch to the hand of Moses, and ascribed the whole legislative foundation of Judaism to him, has given place to one which we persuade ourselves is more marked by a historical sense, and which duly appreciates the principle of development. I am not sure, however, that the unrecognized errors of our ways are not sometimes as serious as the different errors of our fathers. In our desire to demonstrate the religious development of Israel, we emphasize the community of its origins with those of the religions of contemporary peoples, and give all the weight of our historical studies to the pre-exilic period and the struggle of the prophets with the popular religion, whose meaner elements we can expound with an ever-growing wealth of illustration.

We excuse our lesser interest in the post-exilic period by observing that our knowledge of this obscure period is too slight to serve us adequately, and despite the fact that we assign a very large proportion of the literature of the Old Testament to the post-exilic age, we are too absorbed in studying the roots of Old Testament religion to

have much time for the splendid achievements of
its later growth, and too absorbed in the *history* of
Hebrew religion to examine its *spirit* and *message*.
We dismiss post-exilic Judaism as hard and
exclusive, a petrification of the faith that was once
fresh and living in the prophets, and use it at the
best to provide us with a foil to the prophets on
the one hand, and to the New Testament on the
other.   In directing our thought to the post-
exilic period, our four studies may do something
to correct this attitude.

That the study of Israel's mission to the Gentiles
will direct us to the post-exilic period does not,
of course, imply that it had no foundation in pre-
exilic days.   There are passages in pre-exilic
writers that look beyond the borders of Israel, and
contemplate the gathering of men of alien race
into spiritual union with the Hebrews.   But in
most cases their authorship and date are disputed,
and they can only be used with extreme caution,
whereas in the post-exilic period we have clear
and definite evidence of the wider vision that
embraced Jew and Gentile in the Church of the
future.

I

Familiar to us all is that floating oracle, which
is incorporated in the volume of Isaiah's prophecies,
and also in the book of Micah : [1]

[1] The translations of Old Testament passages given here often rest
on a re-arranged or emended text, and endeavour to indicate something

It shall come to páss in the fúllness of tíme,
That the moúnt of Yahweh's-hoúse shall bé
Estáblished at the heád of the moúntains,
And exálted shall it bé above the hílls.

And all nátions shall come streáming únto it,
And mány peóples shall gó ;
And shall sáy :
Cóme, let us go úp to Yahweh's-moúnt,
To the hoúse of the Gód of Jácob ;

That He may instrúct us of His wáys,
And in His páths we may wálk ;
For from Zíon instrúction proceédeth,
And the wórd of Yahwéh from Jerúsalem.

For He will júdge betweén the nátions,
And be dáysman for mány peóples ;
And they will beát their swórds into ploúghshares,
And into prúning-hoóks their speárs.

Nátion shall not lift swórd against nátion,
And the art-of-wár shall they nó more leárn ;
But eách under his own víne shall dwéll,
And under his fíg-tree, with nóne to térrify.

                    Isa. ii. 2–4 ; Mic. iv. 1–4.

This poem cannot be securely ascribed to either
Isaiah or Micah, though both views have been
maintained, and it is just as likely that it comes

of the rhythm of the original, though it is sometimes impossible to put
the accent in English on the word corresponding to that which bears
the accent in Hebrew. When words are joined by a hyphen, it is to warn
the reader that a single accent must be given to the group, and this
warning is given only when the English might seem more naturally
to call for an additional accent. Words which stand by anacrusis outside
the metrical scheme are given a separate line.

from neither. And once it is loosed from them, we have no secure grounds on which to date it. Buchanan Gray ascribed it to the exilic age, while some have carried it down even to the Greek period. It is very improbable, however, that it was so late as this, and much more probable that it belongs to the exilic, or early post-exilic, age. But from whatever age it comes, it brings its testimony to one noble seer, whose dream of human brotherhood did not ignore the true conditions it involved. For he recognized that if war was to be abolished, true justice must reign in the earth, and that human brotherhood cannot be achieved until men acknowledge the common fatherhood of God. Only when men accept His instruction, and His justice reigns in the earth, can enduring peace be secured. No insular spirit marked this singer, for he was not one who cherished the privileges of his faith for himself and regarded all others as without the pale, but instead he dreamed of the day when all nations should be united in a common faith, and should humbly submit themselves to the will of God, since only in His will could all their apparently conflicting interests and needs find true reconciliation.

In Habakkuk, again, we find another short, but familiar oracle :

> For the earth shall be filled with the knowledge of the glory of Yahweh, as the waters cover the sea.
>
> ii. 14.

By general consent, however, this is not original to the book of Habakkuk, but is quoted from the book of Isaiah (xi. 9), and it is once more disputed whether it is genuinely Isaianic, or whether it is of post-exilic origin. The immediately preceding verses speak of the Messianic age, whose blessings are here conceived of as extending to beasts as well as to men. Not alone shall human warfare be eliminated, but the fierce instincts of the very beasts shall be transmuted. It is probable, however, that verses 9 f. do not belong to this oracle, but form a separate fragment. But again, from whatever hand they come, and from whatever age, they clearly envisage a time when Yahweh shall be acknowledged by all nations, and the blessings of the Jewish faith shall be shared beyond the borders of Israel.

A further passage that is germane to our subject stands in the book of Zephaniah :

> Thén will I gránt unto the peóples
> Líps that are cleán,
> That they áll may cáll on Yahweh's-náme,
> To sérve Him with óne consént ;
> From beyónd the streáms of Ethiópia
> My súppliants, widely-spreád,
> Shall bríng me an óffering.   iii. 9 f.

It is again generally agreed, however, that this passage is secondary, and not from the hand of Zephaniah himself. It clearly contemplates the inclusion of Gentiles in the faith of Israel, and an inclusion that rests on the willing consent of the Gentiles themselves.

The book of Jeremiah, too, provides a few passages at which we may glance. The first, which is apparently in prose, looks no farther than Israel's immediate neighbours, and after threatening them with the penalties of their iniquities, continues :

> But after I have torn them up, I will again have mercy upon them and will restore them, each to his heritage, and each to his land. And it shall be, if they will diligently learn the ways of my people, to swear by my name : ' As Yahweh liveth,' just as they taught my people to swear by Baal, then they shall be built up in the midst of my people.
>
> xii. 15 f.

The others look farther afield :

> At that time Jerusalem shall be called the throne of Yahweh, and all nations shall gather thereto ; and they shall no more walk after the stubbornness of their evil heart.   iii. 17.

> Yahwéh, my stréngth and my strónghold,
> My réfuge in the hoúr of neéd,
> To Theé shall the nátions cóme,
> From the énds of the eárth and sáy :

> Only líes did our fáthers inhérit,
> Vánities in whích is no prófit.
> Can a mán make góds for himsélf,
> When indeéd no góds are théy !   xvi. 19 f.

Here, yet once more, it is far from certain whether we have genuine oracles of Jeremiah. Skinner would allow the last to this prophet, but in common with most scholars he denies him the other two, while there are some who would deny them all to Jeremiah.

For the pre-exilic age, therefore, we cannot build securely, though we must take account of these oracles as evidence that in some age or ages voices were raised to declare in these noble utterances that the treasure Israel possessed, she held not for herself alone, but for the world.

II

In the exilic age, however, we have the great unknown author of Deutero-Isaiah, to whom this wider vision is no merely fleeting glimpse, but an abiding experience, giving to his great message one of its fundamental elements. Monotheism is with him sure and certain. Yahweh is the only God, and all the gods of the nations are but dead and useless idols, less worthy of respect than the men who make them. Their worship is but vain mummery, for Yahweh alone is God, the Creator of the heavens and the earth, the Controller of history, and the One in the hollow of Whose hands all things lie.

But such a conception involved corollaries. He who created all must be the God of all, and

must desire the worship not alone of Israel but of
all men. If He has revealed Himself peculiarly to
Israel, then His purpose must be that Israel should
be the medium of this revelation unto all men,
and in this divinely appointed destiny lies Israel's
supreme glory and distinction. Again and again
this comes out in his oracles, in instances too
numerous to quote. A few only may be reviewed :

> I, Yahwéh, have cálled thee in ríghteousness,
> And have táken thine hánd ;
> I have fórmed thee and sét thee for a covenant-
>   of-humánity,
> And for a líght to the nátions,
> To ópen blínded éyes,
> To bring fórth the prísoner from his dúngeon,
> And from the príson-house them that sít in
>   dárkness. xlii. 6 f.

> Túrn unto Mé and be sáved,
> All the énds of the éarth,
> For Í am Gód and there is no óther ;
> By Mysélf have I swórn
> There has gone fórth from My moúth in ríghteous-
>   ness
> A wórd that shall not retúrn ;
> For to Mé every kneé shall bénd,
> And all tóngues by Me sweár. xlv. 22 f.

> Instrúction from Mé shall go fórth,
> And My júdgement shall be the líght of the peóples ;
> In a twínkling I will bring neár My ríghteousness ;
> Gone fórth is My salvátion,

And Mine árms shall júdge the peóples ;
For Mé shall the coástlands waít,
And upón Mine árm shall they trúst.

li. 4 f.

Behóld !
A nátion thou knówest not shalt thou cáll,
And they that knéw thee not shall rún unto theé,
Becaúse of Yahwéh thy Gód,
And of the Hóly One of Ísrael, Who hath made
thee faír.

lv. 5.

It should, perhaps, be noted that in the first of
these passages some scholars take the expression
' covenant of people,' which I have rendered
' covenant of humanity,' to mean ' covenant of the
Israelite people,' in contrast to the Gentiles in the
following line. In the previous verse, however,
the whole human race has been referred to by the
same term ' the people,' in the singular, so that it
probably has the meaning given above here. In
any case, for our purpose the passage is not
seriously affected, whatever interpretation is put
upon this phrase, since the following line—' (I
have formed thee) for a light to the nations '—
sufficiently indicates a wider vision. That this
wider vision is the corollary of monotheism comes
out most clearly in the second of the passages
quoted :

Túrn unto Mé and be sáved,
All the énds of the eárth,
For Í am Gód and there is no óther.

2

It is clear from these passages that the author conceived of the Kingdom of God as all-embracing, including not merely a few choice souls from alien races, but the entire human race ; and it is equally clear that while he thought of the faith of Israel as something that imparted such beauty to his people that the nations should feel its charm and be drawn unto it, he also conceived of Israel as charged with a mission to spend themselves in the beneficent service of the nations.

III

Hitherto I have left out of account the Servant Songs which are found in Deutero-Isaiah, since it is disputed whether they are by the same hand as the rest of the prophecies, and since in any case they carry the conception of the mission to the Gentiles to a new level. I am not persuaded, indeed, that they are of separate authorship, and if they show an advance over the rest of Deutero-Isaiah in the conception of the mission to the Gentiles, it is equally true that there is advance within this group of poems themselves. Nevertheless it is convenient to treat them separately.

Outside these passages there are references to the Servant of Yahweh, but in these passages there are unique elements of the conception. That the Servant outside these four songs is Israel is admitted by many who identify the Servant of these passages with an individual, and when we leave the four Servant Songs out of Deutero-Isaiah we have evidence, part of which I have quoted, for the conception of Israel as a people with a vocation, charged by God with the sacred task of mediating the divine message to men, and leading the whole world into the Kingdom of God.

Into the interminable discussions that have surrounded these four songs it is impossible to go fully. More than a score of different interpretations have been proposed, and of these the one which I have found most helpful is that associated with the name of Principal H. Wheeler Robinson. The traditional interpretation in the Christian Church has been the Messianic view, but to Jewish interpreters, whether in pre-Christian or post-Christian times, the conception of the Suffering Servant seems to have been quite distinct from that of the expected Messiah. In modern times there are still some who maintain the Messianic view; but most of those who find in the Servant an individual figure identify him with some historical figure, either contemporary with the author or before his time. He has been identified with Jeremiah, with Zerubbabel, with Jehoiachin, with Moses, with some unknown contemporary of the prophet, with the prophet himself; but none of these seems to fit all the conditions of the case. Others have turned to a collective interpretation, and have found the Servant in the poems, as in the surrounding oracles, to be Israel.

But since the actual historical Israel does not fit all passages, and is in fact in one place set over against the Servant, some have limited the Servant to the faithful in Israel, or have identified him with the ideal Israel. A vast literature has been written on the subject, and it is probably too much to hope that there will ever be any generally agreed solution of the problem.

I believe the writer himself would have found difficulty in defining with precision what was in his own mind. What he appears to have meant by the Servant was the chosen and appointed agent of the divine will, but the closer definition of the Servant varies in different passages. In some contexts it might be the entire Jewish nation, through whose experience God was conceived to be speaking to men; in some contexts it might be the Israel within Israel, the elect and consecrated souls whose sensitiveness to the divine will made them peculiarly His instrument, and in whom the inner spirit and mission of the nation found their living embodiment; in some contexts it might be an individual in whom the mission of the nation is peculiarly fulfilled. There was a fluidity in the writer's thought that makes all our efforts to pin him down to a single identification doomed to failure. To a Hebrew the community could be individualized in thought in a single figure, a personification of the spirit of the race; or it could be represented in actual experience in the person of an individual, who for the time

being stood for the nation, and upon whom all
its life depended. He did not draw the hard lines
between the individual and the community which
we instinctively draw, but could as readily think
of the individual as lost in the community, or the
community as lost in the individual, as he could
think of individual and community as separate
concepts. Hence to one who was concerned for
Israel's mission, it would be possible to think of
that mission as exercised through the whole
nation, through a part of the nation, or through
some individual, who, himself the heir of the
nation, gathered into himself its spirit, embodied
its vocation, and fulfilled its destiny.

In the light of such a conception a Messianic
interpretation is neither wholly excluded, nor
imposed upon the whole. In general, I believe
the author was personifying Israel, but in the
fourth poem that personification is carried to a
point where it is hard to escape the feeling that
he really thought of an individual, so supremely
the Servant of Yahweh that within the Servant
community He stood out as its representative and
leader, carrying its mission of service to a point
no other should reach.

In the first poem Yahweh is the speaker :

Behóld, My Sérvant whom I uphóld,
Mine eléct, in whom My soúl delíghteth.
I have sét My spírit upon hím ;
Júdgement to the nátions shall he bring fórth.

He shall not crý, nor máke a noíse,
Nor let his voíce be heárd abroád ;
A reéd that is bruísed he shall not breák,
And a wíck that burns dím he will not quénch.

Faíthfully shall he bríng forth júdgement,
Nor hímself burn dím nor be bruísed,
Till he shall sét júdgement in the eárth ;
And for his instrúction the ísles shall waít.

xlii. 1–4.

Almost every phrase in the first verse may be paralleled elsewhere in Deutero-Isaiah, where the context clearly indicates Israel, so that there is an initial presumption that the Servant is Israel here too.   Thus we may compare : ' And thou, Israel, *my servant*, Jacob, whom I have *chosen* ' (xli. 8) ; ' And I said, *My servant* art thou, I have *chosen* thee and not rejected thee ' (xli. 9) ; ' I have *upheld* thee by the right hand of my righteousness ' (xli. 10) ; ' Ye are my witnesses, saith Yahweh, and *my servant* whom I have *chosen* ' (xliii. 10) ; ' And now, hear thou, O Jacob, my *servant*, and Israel whom I have *chosen* ' (xliv. 1).

I have already noted, however, that the author's thought shows more fluidity than we normally allow ourselves, so that while the verbal connexions with other passages are important for their evidence for a collective interpretation here, they must not be allowed to impose any hard limitation of meaning on the word *Servant*.

In this poem there occurs another word of fluid

meaning. This is the word *mishpat*, which is normally rendered *judgement*, or *custom*. Many render the word in this passage, however, by *right religion*, or the like, and compare the Arabic word *din*, which similarly stands for a variety of meanings, including *judgement*, *custom*, and *true religion*. Elsewhere in the Servant Songs the word clearly has a forensic sense, but the religious meaning would seem to be more appropriate in this context. But again I do not think the author would have excluded the other. The whole varied meaning of the word was in his mind, and no one term adequately translates it. For since the word was used for these different ideas, they were clearly thought of as related to one another. Hence the Servant is thought of as exercising a gentle ministry, far-ranging in its influence, whose effect is to bring the world both to *right religion*, which is the source of all true righteousness, and to the acceptance of the divine will or *judgement* in all the relationships of life, which is its expression.

In the second poem the Servant is himself the speaker :

> Lísten, ye ísles, unto mé,
> Give eár, ye peóples from afár ;
> Yahwéh cálled me from the wómb,
> From the bírth [1] He made méntion of my náme.

[1] Lit. *from the bowels of my mother*, but with a single rhythmical accent.

He hath-made-my-moúth as a keén-edged bláde ;
In the shádow of His hánd hath He híd me :
He hath máde me a pólished sháft ;
In His ówn quíver hath He stóred me.

3. For He saíd unto me : My sérvant art thoú,
Ísrael, in whóm I will glórify Myself ;
5c. And so I was hónoured in the éyes of Yahwéh,
And my Gód becáme my stréngth.

4. And I thoúght : In vaín have I láboured,
For noúght have I spént my stréngth ;
But súrely my caúse is with Yahwéh,
And my récompense is wíth my Gód.

And nów hath saíd Yahwéh,
Who fórmed me from the wómb for His Sérvant,
To bríng back Jácob to Himsélf,
And that Ísrael to Hím might be gáthered.

Too líght is it that thou shouldst bé My Sérvant,
To sét up the tríbes of Jácob,
And to restóre the dispérsed of Ísrael ;
But I will máke thee the líght of the nátions,
That My salvátion may reách
Unto the énd of the eárth.   xlix. 1–6.

Here, again, there are many links of phrase
with other passages in Deutero-Isaiah, where the
reference is to Israel. Thus we find : ' Yet now
hear, O Jacob, my servant, and Israel, whom I
have chosen, Thus saith Yahweh, who made thee,
and *formed thee from the womb* ' (xliv. 1 f.) ; ' But

now, thus saith Yahweh, who created thee, O Jacob, and *formed* thee, O Israel : Fear not, for I have redeemed thee, I have *called* thee by name, thou art mine ' (xliii. 1) ; ' Hearken unto me, O Jacob, and Israel, my *called* ' (xlviii. 12) ; ' I have *put* my words in thy *mouth* ; *in the shadow of my hand* have I *covered*[1] thee ' (li. 16) ; ' For Yahweh hath redeemed Jacob, and in Israel will he *glorify* himself' (xliv. 23) ; ' I have *formed* thee and *made* thee . . . *for a light to the nations* ' (xlii. 6) ; ' And all *the ends of the earth* shall see the *salvation* of our God ' (lii. 10).

It is perfectly clear from this passage, however, that no simple identification of the Servant with Israel will suffice, for whereas at one point the Servant is specifically identified with Israel (' My Servant art thou, Israel, in whom I will glorify Myself '), in another he is assigned a mission to Israel, as well as to the nations (' To bring back Jacob to Himself, and that Israel to Him might be gathered '). Those who give to the Servant an individual interpretation throughout, and who eliminate any element of a collective interpretation, avoid the clear embarrassment this passage affords by deleting the word *Israel* from verse 3, in defiance of every canon of textual criticism. The versions support the reading, the rhythm requires it, the sense is in itself unexceptionable,

---

[1] The connexion here is of thought rather than of phrase, since the word here rendered *covered* is from a different root from that rendered *hid* in xlix. 2.

and all that is against the reading is a theory of
interpretation to which it is inconvenient. For, if
we are conscious of the contradiction in first
identifying the Servant with Israel, and immediately
afterwards defining the mission of the Servant to
Israel, the remedy is not to alter the text according
to our ideas, but to enter into the thought of the
writer, and to recognize that essential fluidity of
thought to which I have referred. Nor are we
ourselves always so strictly logical as we suppose.
If I should say 'Before the Church can win the
world it must win the Church' I should state a
perfectly intelligible truism, whose formal in-
consistency is resolved by the recognition of the
different area of meaning of the word *Church* in its
two occurrences.

What immediately concerns us, however, is the
wider vision that passed beyond the borders of
Israel, and embraced aliens as well as Jews in the
Kingdom of God. And it finds the clearest
possible expression here. Israel alone is an insufficient inheritance for the God of all the earth,
and her redemption must be completed and
perfected in the larger redemption of all mankind.

In the third song, the Servant is again the
speaker :

> The Lórd Yahwéh hath gíven me
> The tóngue of a discíple,
> That Í may sustaín the weáry
> With a méssage of refréshment.

In the mórning He quíckeneth mine eár,
To heár as a discíple,
And Í have nót disobéyed,
Or túrned me awáy.

My báck to the lásh I gáve,
My cheéks to be plúcked ;
My fáce I did nót híde
From ínsult and spítting.

But the Lórd Yahwéh is my hélper,
So I am nót disgráced ;
I sét my fáce as a flínt,
For I knéw I should-not-be-shámed.

Nígh is my Víndicator ;
Whó will go-to-láw-with-me ?
Let us stánd togéther ;
Whó is my Ádversary ?
Let him dráw nigh to mé.

Behóld !
The Lórd Yahwéh is my hélper ;
Whó shall convíct me ?
Behóld !
They shall áll wax óld as a gárment ;
The móth shall consúme them.   l. 4–9.

In this Song there is no reference to the mission to the Gentiles, but there is a notable emphasis on the sufferings of the Servant. Here, as in the earlier Songs, there are links with utterances elsewhere, where the reference is clearly to Israel, and not least in what concerns the suffering of the Servant. Thus we find : ' And I will put

it into the hand of them that afflict thee, which
say to thy soul, Bow down that we may pass over,
And thou hast made thy back as the ground, and
as the street to them that pass over' (li. 23);
'It is a people plundered and despoiled, All of
their young men are ensnared, And in prison-
houses are they hidden; They are for a prey and
none delivereth, For a spoil and none saith,
Restore. . . . Who gave Jacob for a spoil, and Israel
to the plunderers?' (xlii. 22, 24); 'Fear not, for
thou shalt not be ashamed, Neither be thou con-
founded, for thou shalt not be put to shame'
(liv. 4). Here there are connexions of thought
more intimate than verbal similarities would
indicate, showing that the author of Deutero-
Isaiah conceived of Israel as suffering just as
bitterly as the Servant of this song, and as being
vindicated and delivered just as surely by the God
in Whom was her trust. But there is nothing in
this poem, taken by itself, to suggest that the
suffering is related to the mission of the Servant,
or that it had any saving efficacy.

For this development of the author's thought,
we have to turn to the fourth and greatest of the
Songs :

> Behóld, My Sérvant shall prósper,[1]
> And be raísed exceéding hígh;

---

[1] Alternatively, we might read :
Behóld !
My Sérvant shall prósper and be exálted,
And be raísed exceéding hígh.

14*a.* And as mány were appálled at his fáte,
(And prínces shúddered at his doóm [1]),

15. So shall the nátions be astoúnded at his déstiny,
And kíngs shall be áwed to sílence.
For thát which hath-not-been-tóld them shall
they seé,
And whát they-had-never-heárd shall they
understánd.

Whó could have beliéved our repórt,
And to whóm hath Yahweh's-árm been re-
veáled ?
53. 2. As a sápling he gréw up befóre us,
And as a roót from an árid soíl.

No fígure had hé that we should loók upon
him,
No májesty or beáuty that we should desíre him ;
52. 14*b.* Márred beyond human-sémblance was his ap-
peárance,
And his fígure seemed scárcely a mán's.

53. 3. He was despísed and forsáken of mén,
A man-of-paíns, and familiar with súffering ;
As one from whóm men turn shúddering awáy,
He was despísed, and we heéded him nót.

But it was oúr sufferings that hé endúred,
And oúrs were the paíns that he bóre ;
Yet wé looked on hím as strícken,
Smítten of Gód, and afflícted.

[1] Apparently some words have fallen out here. The words in
brackets represent the restoration suggested by Marti, and can only be
treated as indicating the sort of line that probably stood here.

Whereas hé by oúr sins was píerced,
Crúshed by the gúilt that was oúrs ;
The díscipline of our wélfare fell upon hím,
And by hís stripes there came heáling for ús.

We áll like sheép went astráy,
We túrned every óne to his wáy ;
And Yahwéh laíd upon hím,
The iníquity of áll of ús.

Though ill-treáted, submíssive was hé,
Nor ópened his moúth in complaínt ;
As a sheép that is broúght to the slaúghter,
Or a éwe that is dúmb before her sheárers.[1]

He was táken without sémblance of jústice,
And whó gave a thoúght to his fáte ?
For he was tórn from the lánd of the líving,
And for the sín of the nátions was he smítten.

With the wícked they gáve him búrial,
And with thóse that did évil at his deáth ;
Althoúgh he had wroúght no víolence,
And there was nó deceít in his moúth.

But Yahwéh chóse to crúsh him with paín,
Trúly he gáve himself an óffering for sín ;

[1] There is a metrical difficulty in giving one accent to *before her shearers*, and it is possible that we should alter the word rendered *dumb* by the omission of one letter, and retain the repeated words, omitted above, and render :

As a sheép that is broúght to the slaúghter,
Or a éwe befóre her sheárers,
He was dúmb,
And ópened nót his moúth.

The rhythmical incompleteness of the line ' He was dumb ' is then deliberate and impressive, and is paralleled in Job iv. 16, where ' And it stood ' gives a similar deliberately and impressively defective line.

He shall seé his óffspring, he shall prólong his
  dáys,
The wíll of Yahwéh through hím shall tríumph.

And after-his-travail-of-soúl shall he seé líght,
And be sátisfied with the knówledge of Yahwéh ;
My Sérvant shall jústify mány,
For theírs are the síns that he bóre.

Whérefore I will-give-him-mány for his pórtion,
And with the stróng shall he sháre the spoíl [1] ;
Because he poúred out his soúl unto deáth,
And was númbered with the transgréssors ;
But he bóre the síns of mány,
And for the transgréssors he práyed.

lii. 13–liii. 12.

In this Song the speaker in the opening verses
and in the closing verses is Yahweh Himself,
while in the intervening verses the speaker represents those who benefit by the Servant's work.
On the view that the Servant is Israel, these are
the Gentile nations, but there is nothing in this
Song taken by itself to compel that view. It is
when we gather the four Songs together that we
learn the full thought of the writer, and none
taken by itself can admit us to the depth of his

[1] It is possible that we should omit the word that is repeated in the
Hebrew of this line, and should then render :
  Whérefore I will-give-him-mány for his pórtion,
  And the stróng for a spoíl.
Often the closing distich of a poem is weighted, either by becoming a
tristich, or by an extra beat in each half. It is possible that here we
have a tristich, of which each member is doubly lengthened, giving
5 : 5 : 5, with a secondary cæsura in each member.

message.   Elsewhere he has shown that the
Servant represents Israel, and that the ministry of
the Servant is not alone to Israel but to the
Gentiles also ; here he is only concerned with the
means whereby the mission shall be exercised.
Already he has sung of the meekness of the Servant,
fulfilling his mission by the silent witness of his
experience ; already he has sung of the sufferings
of the Servant, maltreated and insulted until
delivered by God.   Here he reaches the full
realization that it was by the very power of his
suffering that he exercised his ministry for those
who inflicted it upon him.   He is conceived as
diseased and ill-treated, suffering incredibly from
disease and the cruel hand of men, and by the
nobility of the spirit in which he bore these cruel
wrongs turning them into the very instrument of
blessing for others.

Prophets had oft-times proclaimed the efficacy
of suffering to redeem the sufferer.   They had
declared that God was bringing suffering upon
Israel because of her sins, that by the power of
this discipline He might teach her the error of
her ways.   But here was a new conception of the
efficacy of suffering, deeper and richer far.   For
here it was seen to have vicarious power, power to
redeem not the victim of suffering, but its inflictor.
But this power was not inherent in the suffering
itself, but was born of the spirit in which it was
endured.

The nations were not, indeed, impressed with

the sufferings of Israel in the Babylonian exile. Nor is it probable that Israel as a whole displayed that patient nobility of spirit which the prophet ascribed to the Servant. The actual Israel had not risen to the lofty heights of the prophet's thought, and therefore failed to fulfil his conception of her mission. But he had set that mission before her, the mission of service through suffering, and his profound understanding of spiritual forces was destined to be of supreme importance to mankind. It far transcended any application of it that may have been consciously in his mind, and he bequeathed it to men to be applied in new and even richer ways.

IV

When we turn to Trito-Isaiah,[1] we find a more nationalistic spirit than in Deutero-Isaiah. There is here a fierce glee in the thought of the destruction of Israel's enemies, and of Yahweh as stained with the blood of those He has trampled down.

Who is thís that cómeth from Édom,
With blóod-stained gárments from Bózrah ?
Who is thís so glóriously appárelled,
Márching in the fúllness of his stréngth ?

It is Í who speák in ríghteousness,
Í who am míghty to sáve.
Whý is thy raíment all réd,
And thy gárments as hís that treads the wínepress ?

[1] *i.e.* Isaiah lvi.–lxvi.

3

Alóne have I tródden the wínepress,
For nóne from the nátions was wíth me ;
And I tród them in my ánger,
And trámpled them in my ráge,
And their blóod bespáttered my gárments,
And áll my róbes have I staíned.

For in my heárt was a dáy of véngeance,
And the yeár of redémption had cóme ;
And I loóked, and there was nóne to hélp me,
I was amázed, for there was nóne to súpport.

So mine ówn arm wroúght me the víctory,
And my wráth suffíced for my súpport ;
And I trámpled the peóples in my ánger,
And sháttered them in my wráth,
And spílt their blóod on the groúnd.

lxiii. 1–6.

No vicarious suffering for others is here thought
of, but suffering inflicted on others in the great
day of vengeance fills the canvas, and we feel the
declension from the heights of Deutero-Isaiah. A
harsher, fiercer spirit fills this writer. Moreover,
Jerusalem is the centre of much of his thought,
and the Temple ritual means more to him than the
mission to the Gentiles. Nevertheless, there are
echoes of Deutero-Isaiah's message, and noble
heights are sometimes attained. Thus we read :

I am cóming to gáther
All the nátions and tóngues,
And they shall cóme and behóld my glóry,
And I will sét amóngst them a sígn.

And I will sénd those that escápe from amóngst
   them
Unto nátions and ísles afár,
That have neíther heárd of my fáme,
Nor yét have seén my glóry.

They shall declére my glóry among the nátions,
And áll your bréthren shall they bríng
As an óffering to Yahwéh from all nátions,
Unto my hóly híll, Jerúsalem,
As the chíldren of Ísrael bring their óffering
To Yahweh's-hoúse in a véssel all púre.
                      lxvi. 18–20.

Here it will be observed that instead of Israel
serving the nations, it is these that are thought of
as being employed by God in the service of Israel.
It is not the spiritual service of the Gentiles, but
the glory of Israel that is uppermost in the writer's
thought. Nevertheless, he does retain some
glimpse of the truth that the worship of God is
for more than his own nation alone.

In another passage we read :

And the fóreigners that are joíned to Yahwéh,
To sérve Him and to lóve His náme,
To bé unto Hím for sérvants,
All that keép the Sábbath without profáning it,
And that keép firm hóld of His cóvenant,
I will bríng them to My hóly moúntain,
And gládden them in My hoúse of práyer.

> Their burnt-ófferings and their sácrifices
> Shall be accépted upon mine áltar ;
> For My hoúse a hoúse of práyer
> Shall be cálled for áll the nátions.   lvi. 6 f.

The difference of this point of view from that
we have already examined is marked indeed. Here
it is not the corollary of monotheism that carries
the thought to the Gentiles. It is not the recognition of the glory of God, the sole God of all
the earth, that leads on to the thought of all men
as His people. Nor is it the eager yearning to
redeem the Gentiles from their sin. It is rather the
corollary of the depicted glory of Jerusalem. Too
small a thing is it that Jews alone should look to
this sacred spot, and share the benefits of its
observances and its rites. To so great and holy a
place should men of all nations turn.

It is of interest to observe that in this passage
we have the emergence of the idea of proselytes,
individual foreigners who should attach themselves
to the faith and practices of Israel, and share the
blessings of her covenants. It is far more limited
and less exalted than the thought of Deutero-
Isaiah, yet is it not without significance. The
exuberance of Deutero-Isaiah's hope had faded in
an age of disappointment and difficulty. Yet it
was something to retain even so much of his
dream.

A similar point of view to this is found in
Zechariah, amongst whose oracles we read :

And númbers of Géntiles shall be joíned
To Yahwéh in thát great dáy,
And they shall bé unto Hím for a peóple,
And in the mídst of theé shall they dwéll;
And thou shalt knów that Yahwéh of hósts
Hath sént me unto theé.   ii. 15.

Thus saith Yahweh of Hosts : It shall yet be that
peoples shall come, and the citizens of many cities,
and they shall approach one another and say :
Let us go up to seek the favour of Yahweh, and to
inquire for Yahweh of Hosts. I myself will go.
And many peoples and mighty [1] nations shall
come to seek Yahweh of Hosts in Jerusalem, and
to entreat Yahweh's favour. Thus saith Yahweh
of Hosts : In those days it shall be that ten men of
all the tongues of the Gentiles shall lay hold of
the cloak of a Jew, saying : Let us come with you,
for we have heard that God is with you.

                                          viii. 20–23.

Here, again, it is the glory of Zion, and the
fame of the Jewish people, that is in mind, and
the inclusion of the Gentiles in the community
of God's people is thought to be the fitting issue
of that glory.

V

With Malachi we come to yet another point of
view. The writer of this book lived in an age of
laxity, when the very worship offered to God was

---

[1] Or *numerous*.

but a denial of Him, since it displayed an inner
contempt for Him. People who offered Him in
sacrifice not the best they had, but the poorest,
who thought that anything was good enough for
God, were but insulting Him, and offering Him
a worship which was less than no worship. And
the prophet does not spare them, but cries :

> I táke no pleásure in yoú,
> Yahwéh of Hósts hath saíd,
> And an óffering at your hánd I will not accépt ;
> For from the rísing of the sún unto the sétting
>   thereof,
> Greát is My náme among the Géntiles.
>
> And in évery place íncense is óffered
> To My náme, and a púre oblátion ;
> For greát is My náme among the Géntiles,
> Yahwéh of Hósts hath saíd.   i. 10 f.

Here we have a prophetic syncretism, though
syncretism would seem to have been the antithesis
of all the prophets stood for. For the pre-exilic
prophets had protested continually against the
syncretism which fused Yahwism and Baalism
into a single amalgam. They saw only peril in
syncretism, and would have none of it, for they
perceived that in practice it amounted to the
retention of the forms, and even of the termin-
ology, of Baalism, with the hollow legitimation
that the worship was offered to Yahweh. But

here we find a very different type of syncretism. For the prophet is here claiming for Yahweh worship that is not offered in His name, worship that is offered to other gods. He is claiming that men who did not call themselves worshippers of Yahweh were really worshipping Him, that worship ignorantly offered to idols could be accepted by Yahweh as offered to His name.

I know this is not the only view of the passage, and that it is controverted by some who emphasize that the worship here in mind was offered in Yahweh's name. But there were few places outside Palestine where sacrifice was offered in the name of Yahweh; and if the words of the prophet are understood thus literally, they were never true. What he is saying is that what matters is not the name employed by the worshipper, but the quality of the worship itself. Insincere worship offered to Yahweh was not recognized by Him as offered to Him, while sincere worship rendered in spirit and in truth unto whatever god was accepted by the only God as offered unto Him. Paul could claim for God the worship offered in Athens to ' the Unknown God,' and could declare that men in their religious yearnings had been feeling after God, Who had not left Himself without witness amongst men. And the author of the book of Malachi is here making a similar claim. He who lives up to the light he has is accepted by God, and his worship is sweeter unto God than the worship of another, that falls short of the revelation he has received, and of the principles he professes.

This is, of course, wholly different from the things the earlier prophets had condemned, and it does not mean that the differences between the various religions are reduced to insignificance. It means that the prophet recognized some true worship in religions that he would have designated false, and most modern missionaries would endorse that recognition. It does not mean that such a true worshipper need not be taught a purer faith, or that sincerity of spirit is the sole factor in true religion. To emphasize this factor, as the prophet here did, is not to deny all else.

VI

We turn now to another book, in whose teaching interest in the great non-Jewish world is no merely incidental thing, but fundamental to all its message. With many people interest in the book of Jonah centres wholly in the historicity and credibility of the story, and the question whether Jonah was actually swallowed by the fish; and all the gracious message of the book is ignored in concentration on the vehicle of his message. Small as this book is, it contains a message of surprising richness, and in its interest in the mission of Israel to the Gentiles, it is unsurpassed in the literature of the Old Testament.

The author of this book was the heir to a great

inheritance. Hosea had looked into the heart of God through the window of his own experience, and had perceived that it is a heart of love—a mighty love that embraced Israel and could not let her go, a love that continued to love even when its love was undeserved and unrequited, a love that was strong enough to discipline Israel because it sought her truest well-being. Deutero-Isaiah had carried the partial glimpses of earlier prophets into the full realization that there is one God and one alone, and had reached the heights of full and sure monotheism. The author of the book of Jonah fused these two aspects of truth into one. If the sole God is a God of love, He must love not alone Israel, but all men. It is not so much the glory of God that demands that men of every race should be brought into His kingdom, as the love of God that yearns to reveal His grace to all men.

It is unnecessary to quote particular passages in support of this, since it underlies the entire story of the book. For the book of Jonah is not a prophetic book of the same order as the other prophetic books of the Old Testament. It is not a collection of a number of prophetic oracles uttered by the prophet, and subsequently edited. It is worthy of its place amongst the prophetic books of the Old Testament because, in the form of a story, it delivers a prophetic message, a single message which infuses the whole, and carries its own authentication as a living word of God as truly as any of the spoken oracles of the earlier prophets.

To the author of the book of Jonah the heathen world, represented in the city of Nineveh, filled with an iniquity that cried aloud to heaven for punishment, had a place in the love of God. He desired the messenger of His love to go and proclaim His word unto them, and summon them to repentance and submission to Himself. All the bounds of a narrow and insular spirit are here transcended in this great vision of the love of God. In the final chapter the surly spirit that resented the idea that anything but judgement should be reserved for the Gentiles finds its rebuke in the clearest revelation that the nature of grace is to be gracious, and that if God is the universal God, and also a gracious God, then His grace must be universal. I think the author had himself resisted such a view, until he could not escape it, and that in the story of Jonah's endeavour to evade his mission, and his protest against its success, the author is telling the story of his own spiritual pilgrimage, and his reluctance to accept the grandeur of the message with which he was charged. For it unfolds not alone a great vision of the heart of God, but the consequences of that vision for His people. For penetrating the whole book is the sense of the mission of God's people to enter into His purpose and His love, to be the messengers of His grace, because they share its spirit.

VII

Finally, we must not omit to look at some of the Psalms. Here we are dealing with a multiplicity of authors, and not with a single point of view. In very many passages the writers are filled with an exultant desire to praise the name of God for all His goodness and mercy and love, and call upon men to sing His praises not alone in Israel, but through all the earth. The testimony of praise is to be given everywhere, that all men may know how great is the Lord, and how great things He hath done for His people and for Zion. Nothing less than this is due to God. It is impossible here to quote more than one or two passages :

O Thou Who réscuest me from my foés,
And dost delíver me from the víolent,
I will praíse Thee among the nátions,
And will síng of Thy náme.　　　　xviii. 49 f.

The nátions shall féar Thy náme, O Yahwéh,
And áll the kíngs of the eárth Thy glóry ;
For Yahwéh hath buílt up Zíon,
And hath appeáred in her mídst in His glóry.
For He hath regárded the práyer of the déstitute,
And hath not despísed their crý for mércy.
That men may decláre in Zíon the name-of-Yahwéh,
And His praíse in áll Jerúsalem,
When the nátions are gáthered togéther,
And the peóples to sérve Yahwéh.
　　　　cii. 16–18, 22 f. (E.V. 15–17, 21 f.).

Nor will the nations who hear the Song listen
in silence. They, too, will take up the strain, and
praise Him for all He has done for His people,
and for the greatness of His works in all the earth :

> Praíse Yahwéh, all ye nátions ;
> Glórify Hím, all ye peóples ;
> For He hath mágnified His mércy toward ús,
> And the faíthfulness [1] of Yahwéh is for éver.
>
> cxvii.

> Síng to Yahwéh a sóng that is néw,
> Síng to Yahwéh áll the eárth ;
> Síng to Yahwéh, bléss His náme,
> Proclaím His salvátion among the nátions,
> Among áll the peóples His wondrous-wórks.

> Gíve to Yahwéh, ye fámilies of the nátions,
> Gíve to Yahwéh glóry and stréngth ;
> Gíve to Yahwéh the due meéd of His náme,
> Táke an oblátion, and cóme to His coúrts.
>
> xcvi. 1–3, 7 f.

> Men shall remémber and túrn to Yahwéh
> From all the énds of the eárth,
> And áll the fámilies of the nátions
> Shall bów themselves befóre Him ;
> For to Yahwéh belongeth the domínion,
> And He rúleth among the nátions.
>
> xxii. 28 f. (E.V. 27 f.).

---

[1] P. Joüon (*Mélanges de l'Université de St-Joseph*, v. Part i. 1911, pp.
406 ff.) suggests that when the word *'emeth* stands parallel to *hesedh* it
should be rendered by *grace* rather than by *faithfulness*.

He shall have domínion from seá to seá,
And from the Ríver to the énds of the eárth ;
The kíngs of Társhish and of the ísles
An óffering shall bríng ;
The kíngs of Shéba and Séba
Shall presént their gíft,
And all mónarchs shall bów down befóre him,
And all nátions yíeld Him their sérvice.

lxii. 8, 10 f.

With this last passage we may connect another,
found in Deutero-Zechariah :

Rejoice greátly, daúghter of Zíon,
Shout aloúd, daúghter of Jerúsalem ;
Behóld thy kíng comes to thée ;
Ríghteous and victórious is hé,
Húmble, and ríding upon an áss,
Even upon the yoúng foál of an áss.

And I will cút off the cháriots from Éphraim,
And hórses from Jerúsalem,
And the bóws of báttle shall be cút off,
And peáce to the nátions shall he speák ;
And he shall reígn from séa to séa,
And from the Ríver to the énds of the eárth.

ix. 9 f.

Enough has been said to indicate that in the
post-exilic age, which we associate with an insular
Judaism, there were not a few writers who had a
wider vision, who in the light of their vision of
the greatness of God saw men of other races as
their brethren, who perceived that the grace of

God was far too rich to be exhausted in His goodness to Israel, whose hearts so overflowed with gladness at the mercy of God that they wanted all the world to know it, who felt in their hearts something of the divine compassion as they looked on the world that lived without Him, and who perceived that Israel was called to a mission of service, service that knew no limits, service that should be achieved in testimony and in suffering, and that should be rewarded in the establishment of the kingdom of God in the world.

CHAPTER II

PARTICULARISM AND PROSELYTISM

In the former chapter I dwelt on all the elements in the teaching of post-exilic writers that transcended the narrow bounds of Israel. In the present one I desire to think rather of the particularism I then ignored. For, while particularism did not dictate all the message of the period, the spirit of exclusivism came to mark much of the life and outlook of Judaism.

We are accustomed to condemn this spirit out of hand, and are rarely willing either to understand it, or to consider the conditions which produced it. We have ourselves entered into a great inheritance, for which we did not labour, and we find it easy to speak with contempt of those who never knew our inheritance, because they did not attain the heights on which we believe we stand. Yet it is doubtful if we should have gone farther than they, had we begun with what was given to them, and with the conditions of their day; and it is yet more doubtful if we should stand where we stand to-day, had it not been for that very spirit we so easily condemn in them.

In the pre-exilic age the principal religious dangers lay within the nation. There were periods when foreign alliances brought alien religious influences into the land, and in particular there was the struggle against the Tyrian Baalism in the time of Elijah. There were also periods when subjection to a foreign power brought the cults of the conquerors into the life of Israel. But it was the pre-Israelite religion of Canaan which provided the greatest peril to the religion of Yahwism. The immigrant tribes, regarding Yahweh as their own national God, whose fortunes were linked inextricably with their own, settled amongst people who already worshipped gods of their own. Their religion was a primitive fertility cult, which found expression in ritual performances of an impure character. These performances were observed not because they were impure, however, but because they were believed to be essential to the fertility of the land and all that dwelt upon it, and because it was believed that without them the agricultural operations of the year could not be crowned with success.

The people who inherited this religion continued to live side by side with the invaders, and to pass it on to their children, and when Israelites and Canaanites intermarried, or were driven together by the pressure of outside foes, it was inevitable that the hard lines separating Yahwism and Baalism should become blurred. Moreover, as Israel adapted herself to the arts of agriculture she adopted the rites with which it was locally associated, until gradually a religion, which in ideas, practices, and outlook, was largely Canaanite, but which was professedly Yahwism, became general throughout the mixed population which made up the Israel of the period of the monarchy.

Against this fusion of Yahwism with Baalism the prophets of the eighth and seventh centuries protested. There is no evidence that they were very successful in their protest. There were brief periods of reform in practice, but reaction soon followed. Thus, Hezekiah effected some reform, but it was soon forgotten in the reaction under Manasseh ; and even the Deuteronomic reform, resting on the work of the prophets, and seeking to embody the fruits of their teaching in purified religious observances, does not seem to have been very successful. It was carried through less than forty years before the state came to an end in the exile, yet when we last see Jeremiah, carried off to Egypt after the fall of Jerusalem, he is in an environment where the old pre-Deuteronomic practices still prevail (Jer. xliv. 15 ff.).

I

We have little knowledge of the religious conditions in Palestine during the exilic period, but there can scarcely have been much religious vitality. Throughout the whole period, the Temple lay in ruins, and the country was weak and poor,

4

controlled by the hand of Babylon, and pressed upon by its neighbours.

In Babylonia, however, there was far more religious vitality. Either the exiles had to become absorbed in the society that surrounded them, intermarrying and disappearing as a people, and their religion becoming lost in the religion of the land where they now lived, or they must become a close society, guarding themselves as far as might be from the influences around them, pre-serving their own religion, and resisting that practised by their neighbours. Particularism was the condition of survival for Yahwism in Babylonia, and it was here that particularism began. When first we meet it in Palestine, it is being introduced by Nehemiah and Ezra, who had come from Babylon.

To what lengths particularism went in Babylon in the exilic age we do not know, but it was inevitable that its beginnings should lie there in that age, if Yahwism were to survive amongst the exiles. And of the success of its work we have ample evidence in Deutero-Isaiah, who may reasonably, if paradoxically, be claimed as the first-fruits of particularism. Clearly Yahwism survived amongst the exiles, and to the unknown prophet it seemed so firmly established that it could undertake a mission to the world. He not alone dreamed of the return, and of the renewal of the life of the nation, securely grounded in this now strong religion, that knew how to

guard itself from alien contamination, but believed
that already the shell was ready to burst, and
Judaism about to issue in a world-wide growth.

Not yet was the time ripe, however, and circumstances did not justify his dreams. There was
a return, but apparently of only a small company
of exiles, and the conditions they found awaiting
them in Palestine were depressing and difficult.
Soon the Temple was rebuilt, but spiritual dead-
ness and religious indifference seem to have
marked the bulk of the Palestinian community.
For consider the conditions. That community
had not known the break with the past which the
exiles had experienced, and had continued to feel
the influences which had ever been a peril in the
past. Deprived by the very collapse of the state
and the destruction of the Temple of much of the
form of religious expression, yet, left in the same
environment, but with depleted resources and
influence, it was not to be expected that it would
manifest any great accession of vitality and
strength. Hence, the first thing to be done after
the exilic period was to re-establish Yahwism in
the land, to rebuild the Temple, and to get the
observances of religion functioning regularly once
more.

Nor does this seem to have been achieved with
any marked or enduring success. When Haggai
and Zechariah encouraged the people to rebuild
the Temple, it seemed possible that the day
of renewed national independence was near.

Conditions favoured a renewal of hope, so that the community could indeed take heart. For the widespread rebellion in the Persian empire that followed the death of Cambyses promised the break-up of the empire, and that at a time when no other power on the horizon seemed likely to step into Persia's place. But Darius Hystaspis ere long had put down the rebellion, and established Persian sway more firmly than before. The Jewish hopes had been short-lived, and the little Palestinian community could contemplate no other lot than continued subjection to the Persian power. As a small province in the empire, it would be subject to many influences from beyond its own borders, and instead of the spiritual aggression that Deutero-Isaiah had sung of, it would feel the aggressive influences of the alien culture that dominated the land.

It is not surprising, therefore, that it did not embark on the mission to the world. Nor had it any great prophets, comparable with the figures of pre-exilic days, to give it spiritual leadership. We have the writings of several post-exilic prophets preserved in the Old Testament, but none of them are comparable with the prophets of the eighth and seventh centuries B.C., or with Deutero-Isaiah, and while the book of Jonah, as we have already observed, proclaims with noble zeal the missionary purpose, its author was not a prophet in the sense in which those others were, but a man who set forth his message in the form of a story. Small wonder is it, therefore, that when we come to the time of Malachi we find evidence in his prophecies of lifelessness in the religion of the day. The observances of religion were maintained up to a point, but there was no heart in them.

Then Nehemiah came to Jerusalem from Babylon, and endeavoured to put new heart and hope into the Palestinian community, while half a century later he was followed by Ezra. It will be noticed that the traditional order of these two leaders is here reversed. For the impression which the books of Ezra and Nehemiah give is that Ezra slightly preceded Nehemiah, but that their periods overlapped, so that they were both in Jerusalem together for a time. It is probable, however, that Nehemiah belongs to the time of Artaxerxes I. and Ezra to the time of Artaxerxes II., and that half a century separated the arrival of Nehemiah from the arrival of Ezra in Jerusalem. This view was first proposed about fifty years ago, and has found some support from the Elephantine papyri, so that in recent years it has won a large number of adherents.

Both Nehemiah and Ezra brought the spirit of particularism, and imposed it on the Palestinian community. The former condemned intermarriage with foreigners, because it threatened the purity of religion, while Ezra went further and demanded the divorce of foreign wives. The beginnings of the break with Samaria are ascribed to the time of Nehemiah, though the full break did not come until later. Further, Ezra brought the law to Jerusalem, and while it was probably not the completed Pentateuch in the form we now have, it was probably the latest priestly strand of the Pentateuch, embodying the spirit and principles on which Judaism as we know it was based. Nehemiah and Ezra, therefore, gave to Judaism its law, though not in its final form, and also the hedge of particularism, whereby it was to be preserved from alien encroachment.

Particularism was, therefore, the shell which sought to preserve the religious inheritance of Israel. It sought to shut in the Jewish community, and to protect it from outside influences, that its feeble life might continue. And whatever we may say about the narrowness of the leaders who gave it Judaism, or the lengths to which it later went, it is only fair to recognize that they rendered a vital service to Judaism, and to the world.

II

By many the book of Ruth is thought to be a protest against the particularism of Nehemiah and Ezra, with their opposition to intermarriage with foreigners. This simple story reminds us that in the ancestry of David himself there was Moabite blood, and there are some who think that it is here that the whole point of the story lies. I am bound to say I am unconvinced. For the book of

Ruth has nothing of the air of a political tract, and certainly it is not apparent that the primary aim of the story is to establish that a Moabitess was David's great-grandmother. And if it were a political tract, it would seem to me to be rather on the side of Nehemiah and Ezra than against them. For surely the aim of the book was not to defend foreign marriages as such. When Nehemiah and Ezra denounced foreign marriages, it was not mere hatred of foreigners, such as is fiercely manifested in the book of Esther, which dictated their policy, but the desire to preserve the faith of Judaism. And such a purpose the author of the book of Ruth also shared. For such a marriage as that of Boaz with Ruth would not imperil the faith of Judaism, for Ruth is represented as a proselyte *before she married Boaz*. At the beginning of the story she says to Naomi : ' Thy people shall be my people, and thy God my God.' It is just because it so clearly manifests the conception of the proselyte that I believe the book to be post-exilic ; for, while doubtless in pre-exilic days inter-marriage led to the fusion of faiths, or the transfer from one religion to another, that was quite different from what is depicted here. For Ruth's conversion to the Hebrew faith is represented as something that happened entirely independently of her marriage to Boaz, and in no sense with a view to it. Hence, if the book of Ruth might be appealed to to justify marriage with a proselyte, it could hardly be appealed to against Nehemiah and

Ezra to justify marriage with foreign women of alien faith, such as those against whom their work was directed. For, in its most exclusive phases, Judaism did not condemn marriage with a proselyte.

Hence, while I find it hard to suppose that the book of Ruth was really a political tract, if it were I should interpret it in a directly opposite sense to that commonly found by those who read it as such a tract. I should more readily suppose that David's Moabite ancestry was produced against Nehemiah and Ezra, and the archaic artlessness of this book was designed to neutralize the objection by representing Ruth as a full and sincere proselyte, and no mere Moabitess.

While there was undoubtedly much harshness in the method of Nehemiah and Ezra, it is only fair to them to realize that they were dealing with a real disease. The exiles from the northern kingdom seem to have intermarried with those amongst whom they settled, and to have abandoned their culture and their faith, and disappeared as an entity, whereas the exiles from the south maintained their entity and their faith in their exile. And now an effort was being made to prevent the Palestinian community from sinking, to segregate the community as far as might be, and to re-establish in a fuller ritual the observances of religion. All of this was to the good. The hard shell of Judaism which was being here formed, while it limited the life of Judaism, at any rate preserved it as its precious inner kernel, destined to germinate and burst forth into more splendid life in a later age.

I have already observed that the post-exilic period produced no great prophetic figures comparable with the greater pre-exilic prophets and Deutero-Isaiah. But the post-exilic community treated the earlier prophets better than their contemporaries had done. All the prophetic books were collected and edited in the post-exilic age, and for the form in which we now have them we are indebted to post-exilic hands. Judaism, within its hard shell, preserved these works and passed them on. It was not essentially hostile to the spirit of the prophets, for it sought to do by other means what the prophets had failed to do by their preaching alone. The prophets had sought to purify Yahwism; and Judaism, finding its inspiration in the work of those prophets, sought to purify religion by regulation. The prophets had denounced the forms of contemporary religion, because they were polluted by alien association, and because they were divorced from the spirit of humble obedience to the will of God. When men were flouting God in all the activities of their life, no observance of the forms of religion meant anything. But Judaism, with its fuller emphasis on the forms of religion, made those forms the organ of the worship of Yahweh alone, and sought to impose the will of God upon the whole of life.

All of those expressions of the wider vision, at

which we looked in the previous chapter, are often
supposed to be in radical contrast with the spirit
of particularism so characteristic of Judaism.
Yet Judaism preserved all those utterances, and
passed on the ideals it was itself powerless to
realize. Nor was it, as we shall see, wholly faithless to those ideals. For, while Judaism never set
out in exuberant faith to conquer the world, it did
attract and welcome converts to its faith. It built
a wall around its garden, to prevent the over-
running of its beds by the careless feet of strangers
who prized not its flowers, but it kept a door
through which it could admit friends who desired
to rejoice in their beauty. We need, therefore, to
remember that for particularism there was some
justification, nay, even necessity, and that there
were limitations upon that particularism.

III

We may next observe that the emergence of
particularism was timely. It seems to have come
into being in Babylonia as a protection against
Babylonian religion, and in Palestine as a fence
against the laxity that admitted the same influences
from within and around the land that the pre-
exilic prophets had attacked. It does not seem
likely that it was directed against the religion of
the Persian masters of Palestine, in whose Zoro-
astrian faith there was much that was noble and
pure, and much that appears to have exercised a

quiet influence upon Jewish thought. Moreover, the Persian monarchs are represented as the patrons of the leaders who established particularism. But within three-quarters of a century of Ezra's proclamation of the law in Jerusalem, the Persian empire had been followed by another, whose religion was both inferior to that of the Persians and more aggressive.

The empire of Alexander the Great rested on an idea. He desired to unite the cultures of Greece and of the Orient, and in his marriage with Roxana he symbolized this purpose. He founded Greek cities in the territories his arms conquered, to serve both as the buttresses of his dominion and as the agents of Greek culture. For it was at far more than political control that he aimed. And though death speedily removed Alexander from the scene, he had bequeathed to his followers an idea they never wholly lost. His empire soon broke into warring fragments, out of which there gradually emerged three principal dominions, two of which were cut off from all territorial connexion with Greece or Macedonia. Yet the Ptolemaic kingdom never became an essentially or wholly Egyptian kingdom, and the Seleucid kingdom never became merely Asiatic. Both regarded themselves as parts of a single imperial whole that was fundamentally Greek, and the lack of territorial unity with Greece only served to emphasize the spiritual unity of faith and culture.

It is unnecessary to speak of all the glamour and

achievement of Greek culture, of all the charm and attraction of the Greek spirit. Culturally, Greece far outshone Palestine, but her culture was associated with a religion which was far inferior to the faith of Judaism. Yet her culture was aggressive in the lands controlled by Seleucid and Ptolemy, and it brought a new and graver peril to Judaism than any against which particularism had been devised.

Into all the story of the period it is impossible here to go. Throughout the time that Palestine lay in the Ptolemaic sphere, Greek influence was steadily increasing in the land. In Alexandria there was a large and influential Jewish colony, which soon became Greek in speech, and subject to much Greek influence, and with which the Palestinian community must have had much intercourse. In Palestine itself Greek practice was ever on the increase, and it was essentially amongst the upper classes, and even in priestly houses, that eagerness to assimilate the Greek spirit appeared. Despite the fence that particularism had reared, the garden was gradually being overrun.

It was in the time of Antiochus Epiphanes that the battle for the faith broke out, but much had gone before that time, and Antiochus was but one of many factors that produced the outbreak. For a century the Ptolemies had controlled Palestine, and the quiet process of hellenization had gone steadily on. It had not influenced the entire population equally, of course, and there was a

Puritan party, which clung to the faith and ways
of their fathers, and which looked with disfavour
on the Greek manners and ideas that were abroad
in the land. All they could do was to deepen
their own loyalty to the principles of Judaism, and
to make firmer and stronger the fence of the law,
so far as their own lives were concerned.

Then Palestine came into the power of the
Seleucids, with the victory of Antiochus III. at
Paneion. The stricter party, headed by the High
Priest, welcomed the change, as did also a number
of the common people, who thought that the
unproved rule of the Seleucids would be easier
than that of the Ptolemies had been. It might
have seemed likely that the Seleucids would favour
the stricter party, since the hellenizing party had
favoured the Ptolemies. But the Seleucids were
as keen on the promotion of Greek practices and
the spread of Greek culture as the Ptolemies, and
soon the hellenizing party had transferred their
support to the new masters of the land. Indeed,
they encouraged the administration to increase
the pace of the hellenization of the land. Soon
the High Priesthood became the object of intrigue
and barter, and was secured by the hellenizing
party, who petitioned the king to recognize
Jerusalem as a Greek city.

The stricter party could not but become stricter
in the face of this, and its opposition was not alone
against the hellenizing Jews, but against the
Seleucid administration that was behind them.

Moreover, the grave scandals that made the High Priesthood the prize of the highest bidder, and awarded the office without the slightest concern for the proper succession, shocked not alone the stricter party, but many others beside.

Add to this that the Seleucid rule was far more oppressive in its weight of taxation than the Ptolemaic rule had been, and it is clear that quite apart from grounds of Puritanism, there was ample reason for widespread dissatisfaction. For Antiochus III. had engaged in expensive wars, entailing all his dominions in heavy taxation, and his disastrous defeat at the hands of Rome at the battle of Magnesia had involved him in the payment of a vast indemnity to Rome, under which his subjects continued to groan beyond the span of his own reign.

Throughout the remainder of the reign of Antiochus III., after he had secured possession of Palestine, dissatisfaction was growing, while during the reign of his son and successor, Seleucus IV., under whom an attempt was made to rob the very Temple, it grew more rapidly. And when Seleucus IV. was murdered by his minister, Heliodorus, an occasion arose for it to express itself. For Heliodorus proclaimed the small son of Seleucus king, intending to get the entire royal power in his own hands, as regent for the child. The rightful heir to the throne, Demetrius, was a hostage in Rome, and unable to intervene in the situation. But Antiochus, the brother of Seleucus IV., and uncle of the true heir and the young tool of Heliodorus, was soon on the spot to take a hand against the regicide. But the reigning Ptolemy was the son of Seleucus IV.'s sister, and while his claim to the succession was a very weak one, it is not surprising that there was a party which favoured it. Jerome tells us it was a party in Syria, but it may well have been in Coele-Syria, or Palestine, and have included all the disaffected elements in Jewish society, who sighed for Ptolemaic rule, in comparison with Seleucid. For where interest is concerned, even a weak case appears strong.

Antiochus was successful, however, in eliminating Heliodorus, and in establishing himself as king, at first in association with his little nephew, but soon alone, the nephew having been put out of the way. The gulf between the Puritan party in Palestine, on the one hand, and the hellenizing party and the Seleucid court, on the other, was thus widened. It is important to realize that its cause was not wholly religious, but also partly political, and that the Puritan party was intolerable to Antiochus primarily because it was associated with disaffection towards his rule.

It is true that Antiochus pressed on with the work of hellenization with a zeal that was born of his foolish idea that he resembled the traditional representations of Zeus, and that he was therefore Zeus incarnate, and it was consequently inevitable that he should be specially interested in the religious side of hellenization. In Samaria he met with great success, and bade fair to achieve success in Jerusalem too. But religious and cultural opposition was growing, as also was political disaffection, and each acted and reacted on the other, until finally, when Antiochus was thwarted by Rome in his ambitions on Egypt, he fell back in chagrin and disappointment on Jerusalem, to deal finally with all the hostile elements there.

For trouble had broken out in Egypt, and Antiochus had championed the cause of his nephew Ptolemy Philometor against his brother, though apparently for no loftier purpose than to get his nephew into his own power, so that he would control the Egyptian part of the empire as well as his own. But when the brothers were reconciled, and agreed to share the throne, Antiochus threw off the mask, and prepared to invade Egypt. But the Ptolemies had placed themselves under the protection of Rome, and Antiochus, who had himself lived in Rome as a hostage, and who would not be likely to forget the disaster of Magnesia, was under no illusions as to the perils of an encounter with Rome. Consequently, when Rome's envoy met him in Egypt, and peremptorily demanded that he should choose between withdrawal and war with Rome, and choose ere he moved a step from where he stood, he could only swallow his pride, withdraw from Egypt, and vent his wrath on his disaffected subjects.

It was but natural that Antiochus should at

once strike at the religious roots of the opposition. Even had he not had the intense interest in the religious side of hellenization, he must have seen that if he would break the political opposition to his rule, he must cut away its religious roots. And so he launched his policy of destruction against Judaism. But Judaism refused to be destroyed. Particularism had done its work too well, and instead of the feeble vitality of the earlier post-exilic period, the life that had been guarded had gained strength, and a deep loyalty had been fostered. The revolt broke out, and aided by circumstances beyond the borders of the land, proved successful in defending the faith. The double nature of the opposition to the Seleucids soon appeared, for, when once the proscription of the faith of Judaism was withdrawn, and the Temple services were restored, the Puritan party, who had only been concerned for the defence of their own faith and culture against Greek ways and ideas, were ready to terminate the fight; while those whose opposition was of a more political nature dreamed of national independence, and went on to establish it for a century.

IV

That Judaism came through this peril was due in no small measure to the establishment of particularism. From the start that particularism had not embraced the entire nation, and it is obvious

5

that in Maccabæan days it far from embraced the whole nation. But it had embraced enough to keep the spirit of Judaism alive, and to foster and strengthen it.

The party which I have called the Puritan party, and which was known at the time as the party of the Chasidhim, were the predecessors of the Pharisees. The term Pharisees is not used until later, but the Pharisees inherited the traditions and the spirit of these Chasidhim. They never became the whole of the nation, or even embraced all the religious leaders of the nation. For a laxer party continued to flourish. The ultra-hellenizers of the days of Antiochus Epiphanes, of course, did not continue openly to flourish under Maccabæan rule; but the spirit of accommodation to Greek ideas continued to exist, though in a more chastened mood, and the successors of the hellenizers of Maccabæan days were to be found in New Testament times. Moreover, over against the Pharisees were those who came to be known as the Sadducees. These regarded themselves as good and loyal members of Judaism, but they did not share the Puritan strictness of the Pharisees in their conduct, and at the same time they were much more conservative than the Pharisees in their beliefs. And when we are inclined to depreciate the Pharisees, in the light of what we read of them in the New Testament, let us not forget that they were far preferable to the Sadducees; and when we wish to dub particularism hard and narrow, let us not forget that it was vastly more serviceable to the world than the laxity of its opponents.

Pharisaism in its essence was not self-righteousness and hypocrisy, but loyalty—utter loyalty to the faith of Judaism, and to the will of God as Judaism understood it. It is true that in its extremer forms loyalty became an end in itself, and the spirit of loyalty became secondary to its forms. But to say this is not to condemn outright Pharisaism as a whole, or to forget its immense services, not alone to Judaism, but to Christianity. For, in preserving the life and spirit of Judaism, it was serving the heirs of Judaism.

V

Nor must we forget the place that proselytism had in the thought and practice of Judaism. I have already said that if particularism reared a fence around the garden, it kept a gate to admit friends. Such admissions as were made, were due to the witness of the more loyal children of Judaism, and not to the laxer party. Those who were ready to compromise the faith were not the ones to spread it. It was those who valued it, who loved it so much that they were ready to stake themselves upon it, who commended it to others as a great and desirable treasure. For Judaism did not wholly forget the wider vision of the passages we have looked at, and while it

did not set out to win the world, or send out
missionaries to other lands to summon men to
the faith of Israel, it had its representatives far and
wide.   For, throughout the post-exilic age, there
existed a Diaspora, not alone in Babylon and,
after the foundation of Alexandria, in that city,
but in many other cities throughout the Greek and
Roman world.   Its members did not go abroad as
emissaries of the faith, but many of them served
as emissaries amongst the people who lived around
them.

These communities were in something of the
position of the Babylonian Jewish communities
in the period of the Exile and afterwards.   They
necessarily learned the speech of the people around
them, and entered into something of their life.
In Alexandria and elsewhere they imbibed something of Greek culture and Greek thought.   Yet,
if they were to preserve themselves as a people,
and not be lost in the communities amidst which
they were set, they must cling to the really distinctive
thing they possessed, and this was their religion.
While there were doubtless some who lost their hold
on this, the communities in general clung with
tenacity to their faith, and followed the observances
of their religion as diligently as it was possible to
follow them in an alien land.   They maintained
contact with Jerusalem, and when possible paid
visits to that city.   They did not enter into the
fierce fight with hellenism that marked the Palestinian community in the Maccabæan days, just

because the conditions were wholly different. While there was sometimes a measure of anti-semitism, they were in general tolerated by their neighbours, because they offered no serious menace, cultural or political, to them. But, with all their breadth in some things, as compared with the fierce loyalty of the Maccabæan revolt, they shared much of the spirit of particularism, and strove to keep themselves unspotted from the world. It was just this spirit of particularism, this aloofness from their neighbours, which at once attracted their proselytes and repelled others of their neighbours.

In any society there will be many who will dislike all who are not as themselves, and Judaism has ever brought upon its children hostility on this ground. When Jews stood aloof from some of the activities of those around them, they drew attention to some difference that marked them, and to those who did not trouble to examine the nature of the difference, it would be sufficient to breed suspicion and dislike. On the other hand, there are always some who are attracted by the austerity and aloofness which these communities displayed, and who seek to find out what it conceals.

That some of their neighbours should be impressed by the distinctive quality of Jewish life and teaching, therefore, is not to be wondered at. The loftiness of their conception of God, and the rich ethical character of their religion, would inevitably impress some who were dissatisfied with the shallowness of the popular Greek religion.

Hence there were some who came to accept this
side of Judaism, but without adopting circumcision and entering into the covenant of Judaism.
They were recognized as associates of Judaism,
as 'God-fearers,' but were not regarded as
proselytes. G. F. Moore [1] has shown that the
common reference to these people as 'proselytes
of the gate' is quite unjustified, for 'Jewish law
knows no semi-proselytes, nor any other kind of
proselytes than such as have, by circumcision and
baptism, not only become members of the Jewish
Church but been naturalized in the Jewish nation.' [2]
These 'God-fearers' might be welcomed as associates in worship, but they were not regarded as
within the circle of the true Israel of God. Others,
however, went further, and accepted circumcision,
followed by baptism and the presentation of an
offering in the Temple, and became full members
of the community of the Jews, pledged to equal
observance of the practices, as well as to acceptance of the faith, of Judaism.

In the New Testament we have frequent reference to the 'God-fearers' and the proselytes, and
one verse ascribes to the Pharisees such eagerness
to make converts that they are said to compass
sea and land to make one proselyte (Matt. xxiii.
15). We read of a Roman centurion, who was
sufficiently interested in Judaism to erect a synagogue (Luke vii. 5). From other sources, too,

---

[1] *Judaism*, i. 1927, pp. 340 f.
[2] *Ibid.*, pp. 326 f.

we learn that there was a real interest in the work of making proselytes. Thus, among the treasured sayings of Hillel occurs the word 'Love all men, and bring them near to the Torah' (Aboth i. 12), while Bonsirven refers to much evidence in Philo, in Josephus, and in pagan authors, to show the extent of proselytism that went on,[1] and H. Loewe cites a number of passages from the Talmud and other ancient rabbinic sources, clearly indicating that particularism did not exclude missionary zeal.[2] According to one saying, which he quotes, the purpose of the Diaspora was just to gain proselytes, while another declared that 'the righteous among the Gentiles are priests of God,' and yet another said, 'A non-Jew who busies himself with the Torah is equal to the High-Priest.' With these sayings we may compare the word from Malachi, at which we looked in the previous chapter:

> In évery place íncense is óffered
> To My náme, and a púre oblátion;
> For greát is My náme among the Géntiles,
> Yahwéh of Hósts hath saíd.   i. 11.

VI

Finally, we may note how the apocalyptists took up the dreams of universalism, and wove them into their pictures of the future. They looked for

[1] *Le Judaïsme Palestinien*, i. 1934, p. 23.

[2] *The Contact of Pharisaism with other Cultures*, 1937, p. 41; cf. Bonsirven, *op. cit.*, i. pp. 24 f.

the supersession of the present world order by one in which the divine will should be unchallenged. In the book of Daniel the kingdom of the new order was represented as one that should be administered through the saints of the Most High, and it was symbolized by the figure of the ' Son of Man ' (Dan. vii. 13). It is still sometimes maintained that in Daniel vii. the ' Son of Man ' is an individual figure. But, in the vision, it is expressly stated that the kingdom was given to the ' Son of Man ' (verse 14); whereas, in the interpretation, it is equally clearly stated that the kingdom was given to the people of the saints of the Most High (verse 27). Against this, it is argued that the ' Son of Man ' cannot stand for the saints, because verse 10 shows that the saints were in the vision before the ' Son of Man ' appeared. But this is to ignore the distinction between the saints and the kingdom of the saints. For the ' Son of Man ' represents *the saints as reigning*, after the dominion had been given to them. In later thought, however, this figure of the ' Son of Man,' originally a personification of the reigning saints, became thought of as a true individual, the personal divine representative, who should found the coming kingdom, and be at its head.

The apocalyptists did not build all their dreams of the future around this figure of the ' Son of Man,' however, but worked equally with the conception of the Davidic Messiah, or even without relating their hopes to any individual figure. And in their thought was a real interest in the great pagan world, and in the triumph of the coming kingdom in the incorporation of that world into its spiritual fellowship.

A few passages only can be quoted in illustration of this attitude.[1] Of these the first is linked with the conception of the Davidic Messiah :

> He shall júdge peóples and nátions
> In the wísdom of his ríghteousness ;
> And he shall háve héathen nátions
> To sérve him under his yóke.
> And he shall glórify the Lórd in a pláce
> To be seén of all the eárth,
> So that nátions shall cóme from the ends-of-the-eárth
> To seé his glóry,
> Bringing-as-gífts her sóns who had faínted ;
> And to seé the glóry of the Lórd,
> Wherewith Gód hath glórified her.
>
> All nátions shall be in feár before hím,
> For he will smíte the eárth
> With the wórd of his moúth for éver ;
> He will bléss the péople of the Lórd
> With wísdom and gládness,
> And he hímself will be púre from sín,
> So that he may rúle a great péople.
>
> Ps. Sol. xvii. (selected).

[1] The translations are here taken from the Oxford *Apocrypha and Pseudepigrapha* (ed. R. H. Charles). Where they clearly go back to a Hebrew poetic original, they are arranged to show the rhythm, but otherwise as prose.

Here it is true that the thought is of the Messiah's rule over nations that shall be in fear before him, and shall be subdued beneath his yoke; yet, at the same time, this does not exclude other and worthier ideas. For it is clear that the yoke is conceived of as one that is willingly borne, since the rule rests on righteousness. The same thought of the fundamental righteousness of the coming kingdom appears in another passage, which thinks of its leader as the ' Star of Jacob,' rather than as the Davidic Messiah, though it is clear that the writer would equate this term, taken from Numbers xxiv. 17, with the Davidic Messiah. Here we read :

> Then shall the scéptre of my kíngdom shine fórth,
> And from your roót shall aríse a stém ;
> And fróm it shall grów a rod-of-ríghteousness to
>   the Géntiles,
> To júdge and to sáve all that cáll upon the Lórd.
>   Test. Jud. xxiv. 5 f.

Another passage, linked this time with the term ' Son of Man,' thinks still less in terms of rule, and more in terms of gracious ministry to Gentiles who are in need and distress : [1]

> He shall bé a stáff to the ríghteous,
> Whereón to stáy themselves and fáll not,
> And he shall bé the líght of the Géntiles,

[1] Manson, *The Teaching of Jesus*, 2nd ed., 1935, pp. 228 f., argues that in Enoch the ' Son of Man ' may be a symbolic, rather than an individual figure. Cf. too, N. Messel, *Der Menschensohn in der Bilderreden des Henoch* (*BZAW* 35) 1922.

And the hópe of those who are troúbled of heárt ;
All who dwéll on eárth shall fall dówn
And wórship before hím,
And will praíse and bléss and celebrate-with-sóng
The Lórd of spírits.   Enoch xlviii. 4 f.

In the third book of the Sibylline Oracles there
are several passages which breathe an interest in
the pagan world, but without associating that
interest with any messianic deliverer, or divinely
sent leader from heaven.   Thus we have :

Hellas, why dost thou put thy trust in governors,
mortal men who are powerless to escape the consummation of death ? . . . Reverence the name of
the Father of all and forget him not. . . . When the
wrath of the great God shall be upon you, then
shall ye know the face of the great God.   And
every soul of men, with deep groans, upraising
their hands straight to the broad heaven, shall
begin to call to his succour the Mighty King, and
to seek who shall come as a deliverer from the
mighty wrath.   Sib. Or. III. 545–61.

Wretched Hellas, cease thine arrogance : suppli-
cate the great heart of the Eternal and take heed to
thyself. . . . And serve the Mighty God, that thou
mayest have a share in his gifts.   III. 732, 740.

And from every land they shall bring frankincense
and gifts to the house of the great God : and there
shall be no other house for men even in future
generations to know but only that which he has
given to faithful men to honour.   III. 772–5.

Here the universality of God and of His love finds clear expression, and though, as in Trito-Isaiah, there is also the thought of the glory of the Temple, it is clearly secondary to the thought of the divine mercy, for God is conceived of as the Father of all, and the deliverer of all who call upon Him.

Nor must we omit to mention the author of 4 Ezra (2 Esdras). For implicit in much of his thought, as Oesterley points out,[1] is a spirit of compassion for the perishing pagan world, whose members are more to be pitied than the beasts that perish:

> Let the húman ráce lamént,
> But the beásts of the field be glád !
> Let áll the eárth-born moúrn,
> But let the cáttle and flócks rejoíce !
>
> For it is far bétter with thém than with ús ;
> For théy have no júdgement to loók for ;
> Neíther do they knów of any tórture,
> Or of any salvátion prómised to them after deáth.
>   vii. 65 f.

Dire is the doom to which they are destined, and while it is recognized that they were indeed sinners, it is equally acknowledged that so, too, were all men, including the Jews :

> But whát is mán that thou shouldst be wróth with hím ?
> Or a corrúptible ráce that thou canst be bítter towárds it ?

---

[1] *II. Esdras* (Westminster Commentary), 1933, pp. xxviii.–xxx. Cf. also C. G. Montefiore, *IV. Ezra : a Study in the Development of Universalism,* 1929.

For in trúth
There is nóne of the eárth-born who has nót dealt
    wíckedly,
And among thóse that exíst none that háth not
    sínned.   viii. 34 f.

Moreover, it is held that the Torah was from the
beginning intended for Gentiles, as well as for
Jews :

They devísed for themsélves vain thoúghts,
They propósed to themsélves wicked treácheries ;
They even affírmed the Most Hígh exísts not,
And ignóred his wáys.
His láw did they despíse,
And his cóvenants they deníed ;
In his statútes they have put no faíth,
And have set at naúght his commándments.
                          vii. 22–24.

In all this there is nothing that promised that
pagans should come into the kingdom, but rather
the thought that their case is hopeless. Yet, in the
heart of the writer is a spirit of compassion for
them that far transcends his belief. When he
prays, he says :

Concerning mán in general thou knówest bést,
But (I will speak)
Concerning thy peóple, on whose accoúnt I gríeve,
And thine inhéritance, for whose caúse I moúrn,
And Ísrael for whóm I am sád,
And Jacob's seéd for whóm I am dismáyed.
                          viii. 15 f.

Clearly he would fain pray for man in general, but
dare not permit himself to do so. Yet, when he
continues his prayer, it is difficult not to feel that
in thought he is going beyond his people, and
including also all whose lot is more pitiable than
that of the beasts :

> O look nót on the síns of thy péople,
> But on thém that have sérved thee in trúth ;
> Regárd not the deéds of the gódless,
> But rather them that have képt thy cóvenants in
>   tórtures ;
> Think nót upon those that have wálked in devious
>   wáys befóre thee,
> But remémber them that have wíllingly récognized
>   thy feár ;
> Will nót to destróy those that have líved like
>   cáttle,
> But regárd them that have glóriously taúght thy
>   Láw ;
> Be not wróth with thóse that are deemed wórse
>   than the beásts,
> But lóve them that have álways put their trúst in
>   thy glóry.   viii. 26–30.

To the God who would have spared Sodom for
the sake of ten righteous men (Gen. xviii. 32) he
is appealing to spare for the sake of the faithful in
Israel the entire race of men. For in his heart is a
universalism that found less place in his theology.
All of this, however, falls far below the heights
that others had attained. The cry to God to pass
by the sins of men is far below the eager yearning

to lead men out of their sins to God, and to carry the message of His glory and His love through all the world. To recognize that the Torah was originally given for all men is far less than to share its treasures with the alien, and if the author of this apocalypse belongs to those who embraced in their hearts more than the Jewish race, he was less filled with the sense of Israel's mission to the Gentiles.

From this necessarily rapid and incomplete survey of a long period, certain things will, I trust, stand out. They are that particularism was not born of disloyalty to the wider vision of Deutero-Isaiah and his fellows, but of necessity, and its aim was not to confine Judaism to Jews, but to preserve Judaism for Jews ; that it served a real purpose in the economy of God in the fulfilment of this end, and in the preservation of the life of Judaism ; and that it was not inconsistent with a real interest in the pagan world, or with a deep desire to lead men of alien race unto God, and to receive them into the fellowship of His people. In the mission of Israel to the Gentiles the defensive work of particularism played a part as truly as the noble inspiration of Deutero-Isaiah, for defence offers its contribution to the triumph of a cause as well as offence.

CHAPTER III

AGGRESSION THROUGH CHRISTIANITY

In the previous chapter I spoke of particularism under two different metaphors. The one was the metaphor of a garden, fenced around but not without a door of entrance for friends. The other was the metaphor of a shell, protecting the precious, living kernel within. But no metaphor can do more than illustrate one aspect of truth, and truth is never in bondage to the metaphors by which it may be set forth. Nor will any metaphor serve for ever. The metaphor of the garden was relevant to the period we discussed in that lecture, when Judaism both guarded itself and admitted a steady stream of proselytes. It is less relevant, however, to the position we must now consider, for which the metaphor of the shell and its kernel is more appropriate.

I

The shell had preserved the pure and lofty religion of Judaism through all the perils that had beset it, and at the beginning of the Christian era there was real devotion to the faith within the Jewish community.

In Palestine there were the Rabbinical schools, inculcating a devotion to the Torah that should know no bounds, and glorying in the wealth of the Jewish spiritual inheritance. They eagerly discussed the minutiæ of obedience to the Torah, and were on the whole immersed in the task of enriching their own understanding of the Torah, and their own obedience to it. No spirit of zealous desire to win the common people to a like understanding and obedience seems to have been characteristic of these schools, though they gladly welcomed disciples and gave them instruction. Nor were they active missionary agencies, eagerly sending forth their disciples to win converts from pagan faiths. They cherished the ideal, as we have already said, of a world that should universally share their faith ; they approved of the work of winning converts ; but they did not actively engage in it. They rather conceived the highest life to be that of devoted study of the Torah. It is recorded that Rabbi Jose ben Kisma, about a century after the beginning of the Christian era, was once asked, ' Rabbi, from what place art thou ? ' He replied, ' I come from a great city of wise men and scribes.' ' If thou wilt settle with us in our district,' replied his questioner, ' I will give thee a million golden denars, and precious stones and pearls.' ' Though thou gavest me all the silver and gold and precious stones and pearls in the world, I would not dwell anywhere but in a place of Torah,' came the response (Aboth vi. 9).

6

While it is not fair to use a story save for the particular purpose that inspired its narration, and the purpose of this story was clearly to illustrate the unbounded regard for the Torah, and it was not intended to express any contempt for missionary work, nevertheless it is not unfair to first-century Judaism to say that it estimated the study of Torah more highly than the work of sharing its treasures with men of alien race.

In the Diaspora Judaism had its representatives in every land, and amongst these scattered groups was found a spirit very similar to that of the Palestinian schools. There was a deep joy in their own spiritual inheritance in Judaism, and a willingness to share its treasures with any who sought to participate in them. But there was no great concern of spirit for the heathen world around them. The New Testament provides ample evidence of the existence of companies of Jews in many places, where they met together for prayer and worship, to keep alive the flame of their faith, and where there were associated with them in worship such converts to the faith as the God-fearer Lydia at Philippi. In Palestine and beyond, Judaism still cherished the hope that its faith would one day be shared by all men, but it was a distant hope, and it did not inspire an active campaign to win the world.

I am not, of course, suggesting that this was characteristic of all Jews, whether in Palestine or abroad. An equal devotion to the Torah was not to be found in every Jew. In Palestine there were many varieties of attitude, represented by the many parties, distinguished by their varying views on political and religious questions. At the one extreme were the political Zealots, hating the Roman rule and everything foreign, and professing a devotion to Judaism that was based on no spiritual depth, but on an exaggerated nationalism alone. At the other extreme were the Herodians, politically supporting the Herodian house, and the Roman rule on which it rested, recognizing that the political welfare of Palestine depended on their acceptance of the rule they were powerless to cast off, but with their spiritual vitality sapped by their political outlook, and their loyalty to the faith of their fathers subordinated to the desire to approve their friendship for the rulers of the land and their alien culture.

Of the specifically religious parties the Pharisees and the Sadducees were the chief. The Sadducees were less progressive and more worldly than the Pharisees. They controlled the priestly offices, and were therefore more charged with the care of the ritual of the faith than were the Pharisees, but they were less marked by inner devotion to its spirit. It was the Pharisees and kindred elements throughout the Diaspora who were the cream of Jewish society, deeply loyal to the faith themselves, austerely loyal in fulfilment of the minutiæ of the law, and ever ready to welcome fresh recruits to share their spirit and their devotion. It was they

who carried the real life of Judaism within the
shell of their fellowship.

But the time had come for the shell to burst,
and in Christianity it burst, and its life blossomed
forth in a new eager active missionary campaign
to conquer the whole world. From the start there
was conflict between those who were charged
with the life and those who were the custodians
of the shell—if I may put it thus crudely, and
with over-emphasis on the antithesis. In Jesus
and His followers there was a new exuberance,
which the religious leaders thought to be the
breaking down of the fence around the garden,
instead of the bursting of the shell for the release
of living power.

Inevitably there was conflict. Nor is it surprising
that the leaders of Judaism appear in the New
Testament as the barriers of progress, obstacles in
the way of the kingdom of God, so that many
readers of the New Testament suppose that in
New Testament times the leaders of Judaism, and
not least the Pharisees, were the incarnation of all
that was evil, and that if Judaism can be described
under the metaphor of a shell, it was a hollow one.
We are to-day increasingly recognizing that this
is quite unfair to Judaism, as represented in
Pharisaism. *Vis-à-vis* Christianity, Pharisaism was
indeed a hostile and conservative force. But as
against anything else that could be found within
or without the Jewish community, it was in-
comparably finer, and it was for that very reason

that in the Providence of God Pharisaism provided the preparation for Christianity. So far from the shell being empty, it was charged with a life it could no longer hold.

Let me make it quite plain that I am not engaging in that popular modern sport, which delights to reverse all the accepted judgements of history. In an age which delights in 'debunking,' it is often thought necessary to destroy the reputation of all who have been accounted great, and equally necessary to proclaim the virtues of all who have been accounted unworthy. I am not suggesting that there was no basis for the attitude towards the Pharisees found in the New Testament, nor am I defending the attitude of Pharisaism to the Christian movement. Not for a moment. Pharisaism had preserved a life whose possibilities it had far from completely understood, and orthodox Pharisaism would never have branched out into such an aggressive movement as the Church provided. When Christ and His followers began to reveal the larger significance of the message Judaism had enshrined, its leaders were blind to the testimony to Judaism that was implicit in their work. For inherent in the very condemnation of Pharisaism found in the New Testament is the greatest testimony to Pharisaism. The attitude of the Pharisees to the new off-shoot of Judaism was wrong, but it was wrong not because Pharisaism was evil through and through, a sham and a snare, but because Pharisaism contained so much that

was good and great, because the life that had been
fostered under its protecting care was now ready
to burst forth, and they knew it not.   It is not
necessary to depreciate Pharisaism in order to
exalt Christianity; while, on the other hand, the
free recognition of all that was fine and noble in
Pharisaism does not involve the defence of its
attitude to Christ and His disciples, or imply that
the Christian movement was unneeded.

II

Israel had been charged with a mission.   Her
seers had perceived this, and had unfolded to her
that mission.   But circumstances had not aided
her to address herself to it, nor was she herself ready
for it.   And so, in particularism, she had turned in
upon herself, until now, in the Christian Church,
Israel began indeed to address herself to her task
and embark upon her mission.   For the Church
was the agent of that mission, and Israel influenced
the Gentiles through the followers of Christ as
she had never influenced them in any other way.
The Church was the heir of Judaism, and especially
the heir of its world-wide mission.

I am far from suggesting, indeed, that Christianity
had no message save that it took from Judaism, or
making Jesus the mere product of Judaism.   He
brought much that was new, but it was not un-
related to the old ; and His work was possible
because of what lay behind it, and because of its

preparation in Judaism. But it is not germane to my subject to consider the unique elements in the message of Christianity, or the new Word of God which was incarnate in its Founder. My subject is the mission of Israel to the Gentiles, and Christ and His Church are relevant to our study only in so far as they carried a message and a life which had been received from Israel through the Old Testament and the community which treasured it. If I dwell on this, I must not be thought to hold that Christianity is wholly to be explained by that out of which it sprang.

It is one of the delusions of a scientific age that everything is to be explained by its causes, when it is equally true that causes are only to be understood by their effects. The oak is not to be explained by the acorn from which it sprang. It is far truer to say that the acorn is to be explained by the oak than to say the oak is to be explained by the acorn. For the acorn can explain the oak only when the oak is read back into the acorn, when the acorn is seen in the light of the oak. And when we emphasize that the splendid growth of Christianity issued from the bursting of the shell of Judaism, we are no more explaining Christianity by the kernel from which it issued than we explain the oak by pointing to the acorn.

In all growth there is something new coming in, something surprising and wonderful, something which could never have been deduced merely from what went before. Again and again in

Israel's history something new had come in, some
new understanding of God, of man, of destiny.
We ascribe that something new to God Himself,
for we believe that He revealed Himself to men
who were spiritually sensitive to His influence,
and willing to obey the vision that was granted
them.   Whatever our theory of inspiration, we
believe that in some way these men were inspired
of God, and that God through them was speaking
to men.   And now in Christ, God came in anew, in
a different and richer way, and spoke to men in
Him afresh.   But just as in all growth the something new may be recognized without denying
the continuity with what preceded, so our recognition of the new in Christianity does not require
us to forget that it was the heir of Judaism, and of
Judaism's mission, and that Jesus, for all the new
Word of God we find in Him, was the spiritual
heir of the Old Testament, soaked in its message
and influenced by its teaching.

III

Of the content of the message which Christianity
took over from Judaism I shall say something in
my concluding chapter.   In the present chapter I
want to emphasize that it took over the conception of a world mission from Judaism, and that
it was inspired to attempt the conquest of the
world by those whose legacy it inherited.   All of
those passages at which we looked in our first

chapter were in the Bible of Jesus and of the early Church, and it was these that set the great vision before those who sought to bring about its realization.

In the Old Testament there are many passages which look forward to the advent of a deliverer, who should arise within Israel, and be the divinely appointed agent for the inauguration of a new and splendid age. It lies outside our province to consider the passages which are associated with this concept, but we commonly refer to them as messianic passages. While the use of the actual term Messiah is not characteristic of these passages, it was around that term that they gathered in the thought of Judaism by the beginning of the Christian era, and normally the deliverer was expected to be of the house of David. There were, indeed, other currents of thought, and not always was the Messiah conceived to be a descendant of David, or of the tribe of Judah. In the *Testaments of the Twelve Patriarchs* we meet the thought of a Messiah descended from the tribe of Levi, and the same thought is found elsewhere. In later post-Christian times we meet the conception of a Messiah ben Ephraim. But by far the most important messianic concept was that of a Davidic leader, who should renew the springs of Israel's life and establish a widespreading kingdom, marked by righteous rule and enduring blessings. There was thus an element of universalism in the conception, in that the messianic sway was thought of as destined to embrace nations other than Israel, and to bring to them great and lasting blessings; yet, at the same time, it was a sway that was to be imposed upon the nations by force, and they were to be broken by the rod of Israel's deliverer.

The apocalyptists had a conception with some elements in common with this. They looked for a new world order to arise not out of the present order, but by the supersession of the present order by one wholly from above. They looked for the direct divine interposition in history, for a catastrophic termination of the present order, and the setting up of a régime in which God alone should assume undisputed control, to be exercised through His saints. In the previous chapter we saw that the author of the book of Daniel symbolized this kingdom by the figure of a ' Son of Man ' coming on the clouds of heaven, in contrast to the kingdoms which had preceded it, which could be symbolized only by beasts arising out of the sea. We also saw how, in the subsequent development of the thought, the ' Son of Man ' became not merely the symbol of the kingdom, but its divinely sent founder and leader.[1] The whole conception of the ' Son of Man ' was different from that of the Messiah. Both were thought of as leaders in the

---

[1] Manson (*The Teaching of Jesus*, 2nd ed., 1935, pp. 227 f., 235) holds that the individualizing of the ' Son of Man ' is the outcome of the ministry of Jesus, and that He thought of the ' Son of Man ' as the symbol of the coming Kingdom, until it became apparent that in Himself alone its mission was concentrated, since He alone embodied its spirit.

new and golden age of righteousness, but whereas the Messiah was thought of as a descendant of David normally, the ' Son of Man ' was conceived of as a purely superhuman figure, descending from heaven. His kingdom was thought of as world-wide, but as resting on the divine power that should sweep all His adversaries before Him by the mere word of His mouth.

A third great conception we have looked at in the course of our studies—the Servant of Yahweh. Here again we have a conception which is wholly *sui generis*. It is quite distinct from the normal conception of the Messianic deliverer, and equally distinct from the conception of the ' Son of Man.' Here, instead of one who should sweep away the kingdoms of earth and impose the divine rule upon the world, we are confronted with one who should win, rather than conquer, the world; one whose majesty lies in his patience, his humility, his love, his suffering; whose service lies not in sweeping from his path all who oppose him, but in yielding himself to them to suffer at their hands, and to be crushed by their pitiless injustice. I have favoured the view that the author's primary thought was of the community of Israel, though with no rigidly defined area of meaning; and I have suggested that his thought may not have been the same throughout. Just as in the case of the ' Son of Man,' where the figure that at first symbolized or represented the community tended to be thought of as a real individual, so, too, here the representative figure tended to become truly individualized. And I think that process may be seen within the four Songs themselves. Sellin and Volz would attribute the fourth Servant Song to a different author from the other three, but I do not find it necessary to posit a separate author to justify the development I recognize. The author was carried along on the current of his own thought, and his personification became a person who should represent his people, or who should gather into himself her mission, or carry it to a degree of fulfilment no other should attain.

All of these three streams of thought are gathered together in relation to our Lord. The Gospels frequently apply to Him the term Christ —*i.e.* Messiah—and record that He accepted the term Himself. More commonly He applied to Himself the term ' Son of Man,' attaching to Himself the ideas that had become associated with that term. He also thought of Himself as the Servant, and there is ample evidence that the passage about the Suffering Servant had deeply impressed His mind, and His conception of His own mission. The coalescing of these three streams of thought was of no little importance, in that necessarily, by their very coalescence, their mutual modification of one another was involved.

That all of these three conceptions were combined in our Lord's idea of His own mission sufficiently indicates the debt of Christianity to Judaism for the vision of its own task, and it is

quite impossible to understand the mission of
Christianity, save in the light of the Old Testament,
whose ideas and whose teaching entered so deeply
into its Founder's thought. He proclaimed that
He had come to establish a kingdom, which He
called the kingdom of God. To His hearers this
implied from the start a world-wide kingdom,
such as their prophets and seers had dreamed of.
Jesus declared that the time for its establishment
had come, and that the shell that had confined the
life and influence of Judaism must burst. But
instead of encouraging the hope that the power
of this kingdom would lie in its dominance, and
in the crushing of the nations beneath its power,
He drew from the Servant passages His thought
of the manner of its establishment. ' The Son of
Man is come, not to be ministered unto, but to
minister, and to give His life a ransom for many '
(Mark x. 45). The world was to be redeemed
before it should be ruled, and it was to be redeemed
by suffering.

As we have seen, the passages that spoke of the
Servant of Yahweh were intimately associated with
the thought of the mission of Israel to the world,
and in linking the thought of His own mission to
the Servant Songs, Jesus was giving it that wider
relevance just as much as He was by linking it to
the thought of the Messiah, or of the ' Son of
Man.' While He Himself rarely stepped beyond
the borders of the Jewish homeland, and did
not send His disciples beyond that border during

the days of His earthly ministry, inherent in His very conception of His mission was its universal character. If He thought of Himself as the Suffering Servant, who, by the pouring out of His soul unto death, should release streams of life and blessing, then, clearly, those streams were destined to reach the nations. For the Servant was a light to lighten the nations, and the effect of His sufferings upon the nations and their kings had been set forth as the humble recognition that He was pierced by their sins, and that by His stripes came healing for them.

IV

Nor can we fail to recognize the fruition of those old prophetic dreams in Jesus and His followers. The Pharisees welcomed in their schools those who desired to learn, but Jesus actively sought men. He proclaimed that it was of the very essence of His mission to seek, and He sought men of all classes. He mingled with the common people, even with those who were regarded as the most abandoned sections of the people, and He called them into His kingdom. For to Him the kingdom was not a fenced garden, albeit with a door to admit those who sought admission. It sent forth its agents in active endeavour to gain new subjects, albeit by the gentle methods of persuasion, and not of force. Moreover, its inspiration was to be found far more in compassion and love for those it sought to win, than in the desire to enhance the glory of the kingdom by its expansion.

It was inevitable that the movement Jesus inaugurated should spread beyond the borders of Palestine. At the end of the first Gospel, amongst the final words of Christ to His disciples, is recorded the command, ' Go and make disciples of all nations ' (Matt. xxviii. 19). That explicit command had already been implicit in much that had gone before. He Who had Himself gone out actively after men, Who had sent His disciples through the land in active proclamation of the message of the kingdom, and Who had linked the thought of His kingdom with the universalist passages of the Old Testament, had claimed for the movement He inaugurated the heritage of a universal task. Had Paul not set forth on his missionary journeys, another would inevitably have done so, as the implications of the service of the kingdom became clearer.

What was not inevitable was that the new movement within Judaism should become a separate and hostile movement. It would appear that Jesus Himself did not at first anticipate that breach and that hostility, and it took His followers some time to realize that the Church and the Synagogue had irrevocably broken away from one another. The Christian movement was the bursting forth of the life that Judaism had treasured and guarded, but, since truth is never in bondage to the

metaphors by which it is expressed, the life which
in the Church burst forth in eager missionary zeal
remained at the same time still shut within the
shell of the Judaism that repudiated Christianity.
Judaism continued, as it still continues, a religion
great and worthy in itself, and ministering to the
growth of noble character and real devotion to
the will of God, guarding its own life, treasuring
its own traditions, but not notably missionary in
spirit.   Its missionary vocation was appropriated
by the Church, which regarded itself as the heir
of the promises and of the tasks of Israel, and
which found its inspiration in the prophetic words
of the Old Testament.

The New Testament records the rapid expansion
of the Church, and the carrying of its message to
Samaria, to Antioch, to Asia Minor, and to Greece.
It does not record the first carrying of the Gospel
to Rome, but it provides evidence that it had been
carried thither before Paul went a prisoner to that
city.   It was carried, too, to Egypt, and tradition
says it was carried by St. Thomas to India.   Ere
long it was carried to other lands, and throughout
the Roman Empire and beyond there were Christian communities, actively spreading the fire of
their life and their faith, whether in times of peace
or of persecution.

And in our modern world the fundamental
character of Christianity is missionary, and its
emissaries are found in every land, sent forth in
the name of the Church, and charged with the

specific task of spreading its message and its life. There have, indeed, been periods in the history of the Church when it has sought to make converts to its faith by the sword. But when it has been true to its own inner spirit, it has relied on gentle persuasion, as its Master and His first disciples did. It has gone forth in the spirit of the Servant of Yahweh to seek and to serve, and to suffer even as its Master suffered, that in its suffering it might serve. It has gone forth in the spirit set forth so nobly in the book of Jonah, the spirit of divine compassion for a world that was living without God and without hope. In every age the Church has regarded its mission as the continuation of the mission of Judaism, and the fulfilment of the tasks that were entrusted to Judaism; while the Bible of Judaism has ever been the Bible of the Church from its very foundation, before its own New Testament was created. The debt of the Church to Judaism for the very conception of its universal task is, therefore, one that cannot be exaggerated. Nor can it be denied that the dreams of the prophets have been in no small measure realized in relation to the Church.

It may seem that I am begging some questions in saying this. When we were discussing the Servant Songs in the first chapter, I favoured the collective view of the Servant, though with a definite fluidity, and perhaps progress, in the thought. In the present chapter I have said that the conception of the Servant greatly influenced

our Lord, who clearly felt that it found its fulfilment in Himself, and I have implied that I regard
Him as the fulfilment of the vision. In the same
way I am talking of the fulfilment of the dreams
and hopes of the prophets in the activities of the
Christian Church, when I should not dream of
expounding the prophets in terms of those activities. How far is it legitimate to speak of prophecy
as having been fulfilled in a situation quite other
than anything the prophet could have had in mind?

We do not to-day regard the prophecies of the
Old Testament as verbally inspired, supernatural
predictions, rigidly defining and controlling the
future. We think of the prophets as men, and
therefore as fallible and erring. This does not
mean that prophecy is reduced to the level of a
common thing, from which God is cast out, or
that prophecy must be treated as a merely human
achievement, the fruit of the prophet's reflection.
In prophecy there is co-operation between God
and man, God's revelation of Himself and man's
seeking after God. The prophet was indeed a
man who looked out on the world and pondered
its problems, but he would be the last to suggest
that he found their solution by his own wit or
wisdom. He first of all looked on the heart of
God, Who delights to reveal Himself to those
who earnestly seek Him, and who are willing to
obey the vision and to be the vehicles of His
message. He looked on the heart of God and
perceived some aspect of the divine character, in

the light of which he then looked out on the world he knew. He translated his vision of God into enduring principles, by which he tested the world he saw; and because of his faith in the validity of those principles, he was able to penetrate to the inevitable issue of the events of his day. His vision of God was not perfect, indeed; but this was not because God was unwilling to reveal Himself wholly, but because the seer could not contain the vision, because the eyes through which he looked upon God—the eyes of his own personality— were marred. The messages into which he translated his vision were fallible, because there was something of him as well as something of God in them. To deny that his message is wholly of God, in its form and detail as well as in the principles that infuse it, is not to deny it all divine content. We can recognize in his word a true word of God, though imperfectly transmitted through the personality of the prophet, and just because it is a true word of God, it is relevant not alone to the prophet's age, but to other ages too. For its vital essence consists in principles of abiding validity.

Beyond the immediate situations of their own day, the prophets dreamed of the future glories of the days when these principles should be firmly established and generally accepted in the world, to direct the life of individuals and of communities. That we no longer seek to establish minute and exact correspondence between these prophecies and specific events, to prove that particular words

were spoken with specific reference to particular
events that should happen hundreds, or even
thousands, of years later, does not mean that there
is no fulfilment of prophecy.

On the day of Pentecost, Peter quoted from the
book of Joel, and claimed the fulfilment of the
passage in the events of that day :

> And it shall bé in the énd of the áge,
> I will poúr out my spírit upon all flésh ;
> And your sóns and your daúghters shall próphesy,
> And your yoúng men shall seé vísions,
> And your óld men shall dréam dréams.
> And éven upon sláves and upon hándmaidens,
> In those dáys will I poúr out my spírit.
>
> And I will show wónders in the heávens abóve,
> And sígns on the eárth benéath,
> Blóod and fíre and columns-of-smóke.
> The sún shall be túrned into dárkness,
> And the moón into blóod,
> Before the dáy of Yahwéh cómeth,
> Greát and térrible.
> (Acts ii. 17–20), Joel iii. 1–4 (E.V. ii. 28–31).

It is impossible to suppose that the passage in
Joel was written with direct reference to the day
of Pentecost; since, if it were, it was by no means
complete in its relevance. There was no blood
and fire and columns of smoke, or turning of the
sun to darkness and the moon to blood. But

there was a great accession of spiritual power, a divine exuberance of spiritual vitality. Humble men felt themselves filled with a new and wonderful power, and realized such an outpouring of the divine spirit as the prophet had dreamed of. Not alone on the day of Pentecost, but in every time of great spiritual awakening, there is a fulfilment of the prophetic vision.

So is it with many prophecies. Their fundamental message or hope has been taken up into situations to which they had no immediate reference, and in which they have found fulfilment. And just because eternal principles, and the hopes which are based upon them, are relevant to many situations, the fulfilment of not a few of the prophecies has been repeated, though often partial. It is therefore allowable to find the fulfilment of prophecy in Christ, not in the sense that it was spoken specifically of Him, or had reference directly and solely to Him, but that in Him its hopes and dreams have found fulfilment *par excellence*. He gathered the noblest hopes of Israel into Himself, and gave them their realization. Yet, as I have already suggested, he transformed as well as realized them. He gathered into Himself the hopes that were associated with the Davidic leader, and with the ' Son of Man,' but He also modified them. For He did not impose His sway upon men by force, but discarded all these elements of the prophecies, because He also brought to the hopes they expressed that which

He had drawn from the Servant Songs, and especially from the fourth of those Songs.

It is in this sense that this fourth Servant Song found its fulfilment in Christ. I have said that it appears to have sprung originally from the thought of Israel as the Servant, though that did not exclude an individual who should be Israel's representative, and who should gather up into himself its spirit and its mission, and should carry it to a point no other should attain, and I have suggested that in the fourth Song the author had probably progressed more definitely to such a personal conception. Such an one was Jesus of Nazareth, Who meditated so much on this passage, and drank its spirit into His heart, and Who patiently suffered in love for those who ill-treated and crucified Him, that by His very sufferings He might redeem them. There is no evidence that all the details of the passage were fulfilled in Him, no evidence that He was diseased and repulsive in appearance. But He was the supreme instance in all history of one who sought to save by serving and to conquer by suffering, the supreme instance of one who was consumed by his desire to fulfil his mission to others, and to bring them into the kingdom of God.

The principle that inspired the prophet's vision is one that has found other partial illustrations in history, for others have proved that the love that is undeterred by hatred and persecution, that seeks to serve to the uttermost, even in suffering

and death, achieves its triumph in the blessing of
the very society that persecutes and slays.   The
Christian martyrs, who found their inspiration in
Him and who sought to manifest His spirit, were
such partial illustrations of the same principle,
winning by their patient nobility in suffering those
who tormented and killed them, so that Tertullian
could say with simple truth, ' The blood of the
martyrs is seed.'   But Jesus is the supreme example
of that spirit and that principle, far transcending
the Christian martyrs and all others in the com-
pleteness of His manifestation of the spirit, and
in the significance and power of His obedience to
the principle.   It is therefore wholly legitimate to
find in Him the fulfilment of the prophecy, without
claiming that it was written of Him.

The mission of Israel to reach out to the whole
world, to suffer and in suffering to serve, was
accepted by Jesus, and passed on to His disciples.
He could indeed say :

> My báck to the lásh I gáve,
> My cheéks to be plúcked ;
> My fáce I did nót híde
> From ínsult and spítting.

And of Him it could truly be said :

> He was despísed and forsáken of mén
> A man-of-paíns, and famíliar with súffering ;
> As one from whóm men turn shúddering awáy,
> He was despísed, and we heéded him nót.

But it was oúr sufferings that hé endúred,
And oúrs were the paíns that he bóre;
Yet wé looked on hím as strícken,
Smítten of Gód and afflícted.

Whereas hé by oúr sins was píerced,
Crúshed by the guílt that was oúrs;
The díscipline of our wélfare fell upon hím,
And by hís stripes there came heáling for ús.

Though ill-treáted, submíssive was hé,
Nor ópened his moúth in compláint;
As a sheép that is broúght to the sláughter,
Or a éwe that is dúmb before her sheárers.

He was táken without sémblance of jústice,
And whó gave a thoúght to his fáte?
For he was tórn from the lánd of the líving,
And for the sín of the nátions was he smítten.

To Him God might indeed be heard to say:

Too líght is it that thou shouldst bé My Sérvant,
To sét up the tríbes of Jácob,
And to restóre the dispérsed of Ísrael;
But I will máke thee the líght of the nátions,
That My salvátion may reách
Unto the énd of the eárth.

In Him, and in the far-flung service of His
Church, light and life and healing have gone forth
to the ends of the earth, so that from beyond the
rivers of Ethiopia offerings have been brought
unto God, and men of every race and nation have
come streaming unto Him. But for the fuller

consummation of the visions of the seers, when the earth shall be filled with the knowledge of the Lord, as the waters cover the sea, we still wait. For Israel's mission to the Gentiles, inherited by the Church, is still far from completely achieved, and it is for the Church that glories in the thought that she is the heir of the mission to be faithful to her task, cherishing not alone the vision of the consummation of her service, which Judaism also cherished, but the living, active purpose to press toward it.

I remember reading a sentence nearly thirty years ago, though I cannot recall where I read it, or who wrote it. It ran : ' Old Testament prophecies run to Christ, as tidal rivers to the sea, only to feel His reflex influence upon them.' He ever modified, even as He fulfilled, discarding elements that were alien to His spirit, and taking to Himself only the inner spiritual essence of the prophecy. He released the life of Judaism for a wider service, and took upon Himself its world mission. But He modified the Judaism He released, and there were elements of the dreams of the prophets which He never realized. Judaism cherished the memory of the covenant upon which its faith rested, and the covenant and its sign in circumcision were inseparable to it. No male convert could be admitted as a full member of the faith, unless he took its sign upon him, and this indispensable rite must have acted as a severe deterrent to the flow of proselytes. Amongst the

followers of Jesus there were some who wished
to impose upon the Church this legacy of Judaism,
but they were truer to the spirit of the Master
who discarded it. The spiritual message of
Judaism was more precious than the symbol of
the covenant with which it was associated, and the
releasing of the message from the outer rite
furthered its spread.

So, too, was it with those hopes that clung
round Jerusalem and its Temple. Trito-Isaiah
had sung of those who should be gathered out of
the nations to Yahweh's holy mountain in Jerusalem, to be gladdened in His house of prayer, and
had said :

> Their burnt-ófferings and their sácrifices
> Shall be accépted upon mine áltar ;
> For My hoúse a hoúse of práyer
> Shall be cálled for áll the nátions.

Here, again, it was the spiritual essence alone
which was taken up, and the material elements were
discarded. What mattered was not Jerusalem or
the altar sacrifices, but the soul's attitude to God.
' The hour cometh when ye shall neither in this
mountain nor in Jerusalem worship the Father.
. . . God is a Spirit, and they that worship Him
must worship Him in spirit and in truth ' (John
iv. 21, 24).

The Church was the heir of Judaism's task, but
the task was modified as it was committed to her ;
Christ was the fulfilment of Judaism's hopes, yet

He modified even as He fulfilled them ; Judaism was carried to the world in Christianity, but it was a Judaism that was doubly modified—modified by all that Christianity discarded, and modified, too, by all that its Founder brought into it. It is nevertheless true that Christianity owed to Judaism a deep, inestimable debt, took over from Judaism the conception of her task, and exercised the world mission of Judaism to a degree that Judaism has never attained, and made the heritage of Judaism the heritage of the world.

CHAPTER IV

ISRAEL'S ENDURING CONTRIBUTION
TO THE WORLD

IN the previous chapter we considered how the
Church took over the mission of Israel, and gave
to the dreams of the Old Testament seers a larger
fulfilment than Judaism had given. But Judaism
gave much more to the Church and to the world
than we have yet acknowledged. To the Church
she gave a sense of mission, a world vision, and
a conception of the great task. She also gave in
the noble song of the Suffering Servant a realization of the method by which the task should be
achieved—not by dominance and the sweeping
away in violence and contempt of all that hinders
the consummation, but by patience and suffering,
and humble persuasion. Had Judaism given no
more than this she would have given much, and
her contribution to the missionary spirit and
method of her successor would have been of
enduring significance. But beyond this, she gave
a rich contribution to the content of the message
to be carried. For the desire to win the world
only attains its highest worth when the faith to
which the world is to be won is the noblest and

best.   Judaism brought to that faith a great and worthy contribution.

The seers who cherished the wider vision we examined in our first chapter believed that Israel had something of imperishable worth in her faith, and were persuaded that this should be shared with the nations.   They who created the particularism we next considered sought to preserve that imperishable treasure from contamination, and to share it through proselytism with any who cared to share it.   And when the shell burst in the birth of the Christian Church, it was that great treasure of the faith of Judaism that issued forth to the nations.

I am, however, far from wishing to suggest that the faith of Judaism and the faith of Christianity are identical in all respects, or that Christianity had nothing it had not taken over from Judaism. That would be denied by Jew and Christian alike with equal vigour.   Every Old Testament prophet not alone entered into the inheritance of those who had gone before him, but contributed something new to the inheritance of those who should follow.   And still more did Jesus of Nazareth contribute much of supreme importance.   Nevertheless, He inherited much and made it part of the heritage of the Church and of the world.

I have already observed that there were some things in Judaism that Christianity declined to inherit, and her refusal to inherit them furthered her expansion.   She rejected the mark of the

covenant in circumcision, and she also rejected
animal sacrifice. In Judaism that sacrifice could
be properly offered in Jerusalem alone, and with
the destruction of the Temple, Judaism, too, had
to function without that part of her very being.
But the Church had already learned to function
without animal sacrifice, and to discard with it a
great many of the minutiæ of Judaism's regu-
lations. She took over the spiritual content of
Judaism's teaching, but left the forms that had
become associated with the faith.

Yet, even here, Judaism had prepared the way.
For the Diaspora had long learned to do without
sacrifice as part of its normal life, though it looked
to the sacrifices of the Temple in Jerusalem to
validate its faith, and its members visited Jerusalem whenever they could, and there offered
sacrifice. And, while it declined to admit un-
circumcised adherents to the full current of its
life, it had already learned to give some recognition
to pious and interested sharers of the spiritual
content of its faith, who would not accept its
further demands. Moreover, so ancient a voice
as Jeremiah's had sung of the day when religion
should be wholly spiritualized, when the Law
should be engraved on the living tables of human
personality, and not on tables of stone, when the
true circumcision should be recognized to be
the circumcision of heart, and God's covenant
with man should be found in the inner relation
of his spirit with God; while more than one of

the prophets had taught that far more vital than sacrifice was the spirit in which it was offered. Even in all that the Church discarded from Judaism, she was in a real measure the heir of Judaism.

Nor did the Church repudiate all symbolism in her love for an inner and spiritual faith. She embodied in her sacraments two symbols, neither of which was wholly independent of Judaism. Professor Burkitt says, ' The Christian Sacraments are certainly not part of the inheritance taken from Judaism,' [1] but the statement does not seem to be warranted. For baptism was practised in Judaism before the founding of the Church, and before the days of John the Baptist; [2] and if the other Christian sacrament has no exact parallel in the practice of Judaism, it simply cannot be understood apart from the Old Testament. From the beginning it was linked with Jeremiah's teaching of the New Covenant, and it became the symbol of the covenant of Christianity; while, for the very conception of a religion founded in covenant, the Church rested on the older ideas of the covenant with Abraham and with Moses. Moreover, this Christian sacrament was associated with ideas that centred in the Jewish feast of the Passover. It is generally recognized that that feast has a long history, and that its origin must be placed much

[1] *The Legacy of Israel* (ed. Bevan and Singer), 1927, p. 71.

[2] Cf. Abrahams, *Studies in Pharisaism and the Gospels*, First Series, 1917, Chapter IV.

farther back than the time of Moses. But, whatever its origin, from the time of the great deliverance from Egypt, its *significance* for Israel always
derived from its association with that deliverance.
The new symbolic rite of the Church was different
in form from the old Jewish Passover, and it
pointed to a new date in history. But, like the old
Passover, it preserved the memory of deliverance ;
and if that deliverance was the wholly new
deliverance wrought by Christ in His death, it is
still true to say that all the roots of this sacrament
lie in Judaism. Far more, indeed, that is essential
to Judaism lies in the heart of this sacrament than
in that other sacrament of Baptism, which Judaism
actually practised.

I

The contribution of Judaism to the faith of the
Church and to the world can only be touched on
at a few points in a single chapter. For Judaism
contained much that was unique and of the deepest
value to all men, and, while it has become normal
and natural to us, because it was taken over into
our faith, we do well to remember that it was
first achieved in the experience of Judaism. And
one of the greatest of her gifts was an ethical
religion.

There is no religion which is wholly without
relation to conduct, or which is so exclusively
concerned with a man's relation to God, and with

ritual performances, that it completely ignores his relation to his fellow-man. But religions differ widely in the degree in which they are ethical, and in the range of their interest in man's activities. They differ even in the degree in which their ethical commands rest on ethical motives. For instance, primitive religion imposed upon men the duty of blood revenge. In so far as this practice acted as a deterrent to murder, it was ethical in its effect, but its earliest motive was imperfectly ethical. For primarily it was not due to the consciousness of the sacredness of human personality, or the desire to punish the murderer because he had violated that sanctity. It was the injury to the tribe and to its god that dictated revenge, and the revenge might fall upon a kinsman of the murderer just as well as upon him.

The pre-Israelite religion of Canaan was far from completely ethical. Prominent in its practice was that ritual fornication which the later prophets so strongly denounced, and amongst the very forms by which it expressed itself were these practices which we should regard as wholly impure and anti-ethical. Yet, it believed that in the ritual act powers were released which were essential to the well-being of the nation, and in the name of religion it promoted practices which were ethically evil.

But, while it is true that no religion is without any ethical content, the religion of Israel was particularly rich in ethical content—and this not

8

merely by comparison with the low ethical level
of Canaanite fertility religion.   It is of equal
importance to remember that its rich ethical
quality sprang directly out of its religious insight.
In Confucianism, as represented by Confucius and
Mencius and others of its exponents, there is much
of high ethical quality; but its religious quality is
not notably rich, and the ethical ideals, lofty and
noble in themselves, do not spring directly out of
deep religious experience and profound religious
insight.

Of Confucius it is recorded that his frequent
themes of discourse were the Odes, the History,
and the maintenance of the rules of propriety; [1]
while the subjects on which he seldom talked were
extraordinary things, feats of strength, disorder
and spiritual beings. [2]   When he did refer to God
it was commonly under the term Heaven, which
was a pale abstraction.   He may have understood
Heaven—as the Rabbis understood ' Heaven,' and
' the Place,' and ' the Name '—as referring to a
personal Being, but there is no evidence that in
his thought this Being was clothed with character,
or set an ideal in Himself before men; nor is there
evidence that Confucius was conscious of any
intimate fellowship with this Being, or felt that
his message to men was learned in such fellowship,
or was essentially the message of this Being.   In
a vague sort of way he regarded his mission as a
divine one.   Thus we read that when Huan T'ui

[1] *Analects*, VII. xvii.   [2] *Analects*, VII. xx.

tried to kill him, he calmly said, ' Heaven produced the virtue that is in me. Huan T'ui—what can he do to me ? ' [1] But this is far other than the way of the prophets of the Old Testament.

In Israel ethics and religion are inextricably intermingled from the start, and advance in ethics went hand in hand with advance in religion, just because religion was fundamentally ethical. When Moses went into Egypt and led the children of Israel out in the name of Yahweh, it is clear that Yahweh was a new God to them. It is true that He is identified with the God of their fathers, but it is clear that this was conscious syncretism. The name Yahweh was confessedly new to them, and if they had really believed that Yahweh was actually the God they had always worshipped, there would have been no need for the Sinai covenant with Him. Yahweh chose Israel, weak and in bondage, and delivered her from Egypt to be His people, and Israel in her gratitude pledged herself to Yahweh, and chose Him for her God Who had first chosen her for His people. The religious bond that united Israel and Yahweh was a covenant bond, and it rested on the ethical emotion of gratitude. Of the theological consequences of this experience I shall say something below, but here it is relevant to observe that a religion which was adopted under the constraint of gratitude was ethically based from the beginning.

Let me hasten to add that I do not believe all

[1] *Analects*, VII. xxii.

the Israelite tribes were with Moses, or shared in this covenant. I do not think they all adopted Yahwism in the same way, or at the same time.[1] I believe that Yahwism had already begun to permeate some of the Israelite tribes, which did not go down into Egypt, even before the days of Moses. But, under the stimulus of his great personality, and of the ever-memorable experience of the Exodus, the worship of Yahweh in the tribes Moses led was established on a worthier basis, and was enriched in itself, and ultimately passed its higher quality to the sister tribes. In its primitive character Yahwism does not seem to have been notably different from other contemporary faiths, but, as it came through Moses into the tribes he led, it gained a new quality.

That ethical quality was developed by the prophets. It is common to recognize that Israel was not alone in having prophets, ecstatics who were seized by divine power, and made the messengers of the divine will to their fellows. We are reminded that the story of Wen-amon, and the account of the prophets of Baal on Mount Carmel in the contest with Elijah, attest their existence outside Yahwism. But from the start Hebrew prophecy struck an ethical note which is not attested elsewhere. When David committed adultery with Bathsheba, and then treacherously had her loyal husband put out of the way, it was a prophet who went to him with a fearless ' Thou

[1] Cf. my *Israel's Sojourn in Egypt*, Manchester University Press, 1938.

art the man,' to rebuke him. When Ahab suffered
Jezebel to have Naboth judicially murdered, it
was another prophet who drove home by his
parable of the widow's ewe lamb the condemnation
of the act. But neither of these prophets spoke
merely as the mouthpiece of the popular con-
science. It was in the name of God that they
spoke, claiming to be His messengers, and making
their demand for worthier conduct in His name,
and as the demand of religion upon the king.
Few were the countries in that age where any
subject dared to utter so direct and severe a
judgement upon his king, and in far more recent
ages the sins of kings and of nobles have been
accepted with a resignation that was alien to
Israel's prophets.

The eighth-century prophets carried the work
of ethicizing religion a great deal further. To
them the violation of the principles of religion lay
not alone in neglecting the observances of religion,
or violating the specific commands of accepted
law. For the strong to take advantage of the
weak and to oppress the weak, or to be hard and
selfish in dealing with those who lay in their
power, was an offence that made of none effect
the most elaborate correctness in all the ritual
observances of religion. And again this message
came not as the revolt of the human spirit against
a hollow and impotent religion, but as the inner
voice of that religion unfolding a deeper understanding of its spirit, and speaking in the name of

its God. The word of the prophets was ever
based on their vision of God, and in Israel the
revolt against the religion of the hour ever led to
a deeper religion, not to the sweeping away of
religion. The prophets recognized the rights of
man, and championed them, just because they saw
him as a child of God. They did not think of his
rights as inherently his in virtue of what he was
in himself, but as his because God in His grace
had decreed them for him. They championed
righteousness, not because they were thinkers who
had found a philosophical basis for it, but because
they realized that God was righteous, and therefore all that was not righteous was an offence to
Him and a denial of Him.

They were led, indeed, beyond the conception
of righteousness to the conception of sympathy,
love, grace, as the spring of conduct, and in the
book of Deuteronomy this spirit is inculcated
again and again. In Eastern lands to-day men are
impressed with the philanthropic works of the
Christian Church. They observe that wherever
the Christian faith penetrates hospitals, orphanages,
and other gracious agencies spring up; that in
times of flood and famine the Christian representatives are eager to carry relief wherever they can.
People who themselves repudiate the Christian
faith are so impressed with this spirit that they
are seeking to graft it upon their own faiths. We
think of the virtue of sympathy as a specifically
Christian virtue, and certainly in Christianity it

has produced fruits unparalleled elsewhere. It expresses itself in a thousand ways. In India it expressed itself more than a century ago in the effective protest against the burning of widows. In China it expressed itself in the protest against foot-binding; and to-day so influential a non-Christian leader as Hu Shih confesses that Chinese society stands condemned by the fact that for a thousand years no voice was raised against this inhuman practice. But whence did Christianity get this great virtue, which it has striven so largely to express? Whence, but in its heritage from Judaism? There was sympathy and kindness in the world outside Judaism, of course. But nowhere was it so exalted and honoured. Nowhere was it made one of the very corollaries of faith—nay, rather, one of the corollaries of the vision of God. It was because God was recognized to be a God of grace, bounteous and merciful, that men were summoned to display a like spirit.

II

Another great gift of Judaism was her recognition of history and experience as the vehicle of revelation. Judaism was not based on Nature or mythology, nor was it primarily a speculative religion; it rested not on fear or on superstition, but was firmly based on experience. I do not wish to deny, of course, that lying behind the Old Testament, and often appearing through it, can be traced a mythology and a superstition falling far short of what I am discussing. It is when we look back over Judaism in the light of what it became that we can see what is its essential spirit, and we observe that all that was distinctively its own came to it through history and experience. It was never merely a collection of principles, and beliefs, and practices, floating in the void. Everything went back to experience, and all was real as experience itself.

Israel believed that God was a gracious deliverer, not because this was the highest conception she could attain, but because He had delivered her in an amazing way in the Exodus. He had taken a people that had never worshipped Him, and had brought them out from Egypt. That experience of deliverance was certain and unforgettable, and it had been wrought through the hand of Moses, who claimed that he was acting in the name of Yahweh and under His direction. Israel, that was in no doubt of the experience, accepted the explanation, and it would be hard to suggest one more relevant or more reasonable. But, if this was the act of Yahweh, then by the same token it was a revelation of His character.

The prophets constantly represented history as the sphere of Yahweh's activity. He controlled its movements, and made it serve His purposes. Kings and nations were never regarded as mere puppets in His hand, without responsibility for their acts. They were free agents, working out the purposes of their own hearts, yet at the same time there were bounds they could not overstep, and He Who makes the wrath of men to praise Him turned their very purposes to the fulfilment of His purposes. The prophets never pretended that everything that happened was God's will. They protested that a great deal that happened was not His will, but its antithesis. Yet, the very turbulent forces that were proudly antagonistic to His will could be used by Him to discipline others, and contained the seeds of their own undoing and destruction. When the prophets looked out on the world and saw evil flourishing around them, evil that was an offence against God, it seemed to them to cry out to Heaven for punishment, that by discipline the evil might be exorcized. And when Israel was caught in the clash of empires, they saw the hand of God. Their deepest interest was in the message to Israel of her national experiences, what God was trying to say to her through her history, and they sought to help her to gather from the experience, however dark and bitter it might be, something that would enrich her spirit. Here was a noble attitude to history that has never been transcended, the firm faith that through all the policies of men, for which men alone and not God are responsible, God is yet speaking.

Nor was it through national experience alone that God spake to men. Through the individual experience He speaks to the individual, and often utters a word of wider than individual significance. But He can declare His will only in so far as men are willing to hear it. Hosea married a partner who was faithless to him, and it became of deep significance in the history of religion. Others have known faithless partners, without finding any blessing for themselves or for others in the experience. For it is not the experience of itself that enriches. It is God Who turns it to the enrichment of those who are teachable. Hosea found in the tragedy of his own home, and in the unquenchable love of his own heart for his faithless wife, a new understanding of the character of God, and a deeper penetration into the nature of human sin as an outrage upon love. His message was not born in the study. It was born in experience; and the very experience that cut like a knife into his heart, with a like vividness and certainty, brought him the revelation of God.

Jeremiah did not attain his understanding of the inwardness of true religion by quiet and leisured meditation. He was himself the loneliest of men; without a wife, hated of his family, persecuted, misunderstood, sometimes imprisoned and shut off from the observances of religion, he was cast back upon God, and found in his soul's intercourse with God a spring of life and refreshment. He knew God with the immediacy of experience, knew that true worship was independent of the Temple, or of any material thing, knew it with a certainty that nothing could rob him of; and it was this that gave conviction and force to his message to men.

Or again, how did Israel attain the belief in the doctrine of the resurrection ? Not along the way of speculation on the mysteries of being, but in the crucible of experience. The author of the book of Job in a daring moment came to the verge of the belief, though elsewhere he displays only the usual contemporary belief in a shadowy existence after death, where a man is isolated from God, and ignorant of all that goes on in the universe, conscious only of his deep misery. It is commonly believed that the author of Job is not a detached student of the problem with which he wrestles, but one who had himself tasted deeply of the suffering he describes, one whose own soul had passed through all the torturing questionings that bitter experience had raised. His great message was based on a profound experience, and it led him to the verge of the faith that death should not for ever isolate him from God, but that he should be conscious of his vindication.

The fullest and clearest declaration of faith in the resurrection is found in the book of Daniel, and again it was born of experience. In the terrible days of the Maccabæan persecution, the author of this book heartened his fellows for the struggle by his stories of Daniel and his companions, who refused to be faithless to their God and to the claims of their religion, and who were delivered by the power of God. He assured them

by his visions that triumph was certain, and that
the kingdom should be given to the saints. But
the plain and undeniable fact was that many lost
their lives in that struggle. In the stories Daniel
and his companions were delivered from beasts
and from flames, but in the grim facts of the
Maccabæan struggle many of the faithful perished,
as did those who refused to violate the Sabbath
by their own defence (1 Macc. ii. 29–38).
Shadrach, Meshach, and Abed-nego are represented as saying, ' Our God . . . is able to deliver
us . . . and he will deliver us ; but if not . . . we
will not serve thy gods ' (Dan. iii. 17 f.); and in
these Maccabæan days not a few rose to the same
heights of loyalty, and were not delivered. Hence,
though the kingdom should be given to the saints
who survived, of what profit could this be to those
whose sufferings and whose sacrifices had contributed to the victory ? Surely they could not be
shut out from the glories of the coming kingdom,
but must be raised to share with those who
survived its enduring blessings. And similarly
some of their adversaries, who had found a swift
death ere the struggle ended, surely deserved some
deeper agony as the reward of their iniquity, and
must be raised to experience it. It was not,
therefore, abstract speculation that brought this
author to his faith in the resurrection, but reflection
on the great and terrible experiences through
which he had lived, and the inner dynamic of his
own earlier messages. He was profoundly con-

vinced that the power of God was great enough to have delivered His servants, and that the justice of God could not exclude from a share in the blessings those whose loyalty was so conspicuous. If He had not delivered them, it must be because He purposed a yet more striking demonstration of His approval, and a yet more wonderful deliverance.

Judaism is a religion rooted and grounded in history, and it regarded history as the sphere of divine activity, and both corporate and individual experience as the vehicle of revelation. And Christianity inherited the same characteristic. It, too, is rooted in history, in all the history of Israel, and in the experience of Jesus of Nazareth. It, too, believes that God is revealed in human experience, and it finds the supreme revelation of God in a historical event—in the Cross of Christ. It has ever taught men to gather the lessons of their experience, and by humble sensitiveness to the voice of God to learn what He is saying to them through their experiences. It has taught that He controls all human history, and speaks to nations through collective experience, warning and disciplining by suffering, encouraging faith by His deliverance, revealing to men the immutable character of His own heart, and the principles whereby alone nations can truly live, through concrete and living experience. Of greater moment than experience is the message of experience; and in directing men and nations to

seek that message, Judaism has rendered a vast
service to the world, which the world has still far
from completely apprehended.

III

Moreover, in her exalted theology Israel offered
a great and worthy contribution. She did not
begin with the full conception of monotheism,
but she came to attain it; and long before she
attained that, she had attained much that was of
equal importance. For the character of God is
of no less importance than His unity.

We are accustomed to think of the characteristic
teaching of Christianity about God as lying in the
thought of His Fatherhood and love. But the
Fatherhood of God is taught in the Old Testament
as well as the New. 'And now, Yahweh, thou
art our father' is the cry of an Old Testament
writer (Isa. lxiv. 8), as is the familiar 'Like as a
father pitieth his children, so Yahweh pitieth them
that fear him' (Ps. ciii. 13), while Hosea declared
the same truth from the other side, 'When Israel
was a child, then I loved him, and called my son
out of Egypt' (Hos. xi. 1). And if 'God is love'
is a New Testament text, its truth was perceived
by Hosea and the author of Jonah, and many
another Old Testament writer.

Nor did Israel, in all her teaching of the grace
of God, ever lose sight of His majesty and glory
and exalted character. She was never beguiled

into an easy familiarity with Him, but preserved a reverence that was born of the sense of His difference from us, as well as His kinship with us. He is high above us, as Isaiah perceived in the moment of his call; and if His love calls forth our love in response, His greatness equally calls forth our deepest awe. That awe is not a fear which is based on the arbitrariness of His power, however, and the uncertainty how it will break out next, for His power is matched with His goodness, His justice, and the dependableness of His character. He demands of men justice and righteousness in the relations of their life just because He is just and righteous Himself. He reveals the goodness He asks, and only desires that men should reflect in their lives something of the quality of His own character. For right is right, not because it is laid down by God and prescribed for us by Him, but because it accords with what God is in Himself.

Moreover, He is a redeeming God. From the beginning of her experience Israel realized this. For He had redeemed her from Egypt. And in the course of her growth Israel came to realize that He who had delivered from human oppressors was ever seeking to effect the deeper deliverance from all that was evil and hateful to Him. For Israel developed a great conception not alone of God but of man, and a deep penetration into the nature of sin and its exceeding sinfulness. To her it was not alone an offence against God, but an offence against the sinner himself, marring the

very work of God in him. It lay in yielding to
whatever is alien to the character of God, and its
real atonement lay less in placating an angry God
than in the creation in the sinner of a clean heart
and the renewal of a right spirit within him. And
this is a work that God alone can achieve, and that
it is His nature to achieve. But He is a God Who
respects human freedom. There are limits beyond
which human freedom cannot go ; but, on the other
hand, there are limits beyond which God Himself
does not pass to coerce His creatures. I know
there is a doctrine of election running through the
Old Testament, but it would not be untrue to
express it in the form ' God chooses those who
respond to His choice.' The freedom of the
response is as firmly held as the assurance that the
initiative is God's.

Much else is in the thought of God in the Old
Testament. Of His purpose for the world, and
His desire that His own should be the instrument
of His purpose, entering into it and sharing it
with Him, much has been said in the course of
these studies. And the overwhelming sense of
the reality of God has already appeared. To Israel
He was not a pale shadow, but a sure reality, just
because He was found in living experience. It is
true that even to primitive people the gods may
be intensely real, but there the sense of reality is
commonly born of fear, fear of the malign influences that surround men, and of the impossi-
bility of knowing their attitude with security.

But Israel's sense of the reality of God was quite other than this. For it was born of her experience of Him.

All of this Judaism preserved to be inherited by the Church, and to be carried to the nations by the Church. For all of this is no less true of Christianity than it is of Judaism. But Christianity did not need to achieve this faith herself. It was already achieved for her in Israel.

IV

Not less is the debt of the Church to Israel for her spiritual worship. In the Old Testament the centre of religion is the Temple—or in pre-exilic days the multiplicity of shrines that abounded in the land. In the later law of the post-exilic age, when the Jerusalem Temple stood without rival, save in the Samaritan shrine, the splendid ritual of the sacrifices occupies pride of place. But we know from the work of the Chronicler, and from the Psalter, that music and song occupied an important place in the worship of the Temple. From the book of Jeremiah, and from the New Testament, we know that addresses could be given to the people in the Temple courts, but the addresses of which we have record were unofficial addresses, uttered by persons in the crowd in the Temple court to those who gathered round them. They were not in any sense the organ of the worship of the Temple. In all this there is nothing

unique, save the unique collection of Songs which
has come down to us in the Psalter, and the rich
liturgical element of the Temple worship which
seems to have grown up. And if Judaism had
given us nothing but the Psalter, our debt would
still have been inexpressibly great. But she
contributed much more than that to our worship.

I shall never forget the impression made upon
me when I first stood in a pagan shrine in China.
Within a large courtyard I found some tiny
shrines, no larger than the rooms of an ordinary
house, and each of these was more than half-
filled with the table on which stood the idols. I
realized, as I had never realized from anything I
had read, that anything like worship in our sense
of the word was impossible, and that worshippers
must come singly to place their incense before the
gods, do their obeisance, and leave their coin.
On feast days, when numbers attended the shrine,
there might be fellowship in the courtyard, but
there could be none in the act of worship. I had
been before into Mohammedan mosques, where
the differences from our Churches are less striking.
But Islam is in some measure the heir of Judaism,
and for her form of worship she, no less than
Christianity, owes a debt to the Jews. For it was
Judaism that created the form of worship which,
in differing ways, has been adopted and adapted in
Christianity and in Islam.

In the New Testament we find the Synagogue
the centre of much of the religious life of Judaism,

and the Synagogue stood beside the Temple as an organ of religious worship. Probably the first beginnings of the Synagogue had been in Babylonia, in the period of the Exile, when the Jews in an alien land, cut off from the Temple and the forms of worship they had known, gathered together to sing the songs of Zion in a strange land, and to keep alive in one another's hearts the faith they had imperfectly kept in their own land.

The Synagogue had developed, and by the beginning of the Christian era had become an established feature of Judaism, both in Palestine and in the Diaspora. Its worship included the reading of the Scriptures of the Old Testament and prayer, together with exposition of the Scriptures, though this last was probably not an invariable part of the service. There was no animal sacrifice here, and no elaborate ritual. For, fundamentally, the simple service of the Synagogue existed to provide the Jew with an opportunity for corporate worship, and to remind him of the sacred treasure of his faith, and its obligations. It familiarized him with the Scriptures and with the content of his faith, and fostered in him the spirit of worship.

In this there was something unique and of enduring significance. It was other than the Greek schools, where men gathered to study and to discuss philosophy and religion. In the Synagogue, religion was not only discussed, but practised, and it fostered not merely an intellectual understanding of the faith of Judaism, but the spirit of humble obedience to the demands of the faith. For it was essentially and fundamentally the organ of spiritual worship, the united out-pouring of the spirit before God in prayer, the united attention to the Word of God, and the united acceptance of the claims of the faith. It is true, as Jeremiah had realized, that the individual soul can worship God wherever it may be. But it is also true that there is a value in corporate worship, when each contributes something to the spirit of the worship, and receives back from that spirit something far greater for the enrichment of his own spirit. It was Judaism that discovered and fostered this, and passed it on to the Church.

There were doubtless other groups to be found in the days of the Roman Empire, where men gathered to perform religious rites and to teach the mysteries of their faith. Some of these may also have owed something to the Synagogue, indeed; but, in any case, they have long since passed away, leaving no abiding contribution to the enrichment of mankind. In Church and Mosque and Synagogue men still assemble for spiritual worship, and all three run back to the Jewish Synagogue of early Judaism.

V

Finally, in the imperishable literature of the Old Testament Israel has offered to the Church and to the world a magnificent and an enduring contribution. So long as human speech endures, this collection will be treasured, and will continue to minister to the spirit of man. Of its range and variety, its superb literary value, and its robustness of spirit, nothing need here be said. It is a record of human experience, and it is relevant to human need in every situation, and through it all there is a spiritual penetration of the deepest value. It tells how men heard God speaking in all that they passed through, and how they came to understand the nature of God and the meaning of life.

In modern times our study of the Old Testament has undergone a great change. We have realized something of the complex literary processes which lie behind the books it contains; and from being regarded as a purely supernatural production it has come to be thought of as a human achievement. Its historical records and its ancient stories have been closely and critically examined, and are no longer regarded as infallibly accurate, and there are not a few who think it has been discredited on this side. All of this, coupled with the increased difficulty of understanding the Old Testament in the light of modern knowledge and modern study, has combined to bring about its relative neglect.

Moreover, there are some who, on other grounds, advocate its neglect. They direct attention to the lower levels of its thought and teaching, and regard it as a spiritual peril. It contains so much that is sub-Christian, they remind us, so much that has been discarded in Christianity, or that is irrelevant to the Christian believer, and they would deliver the Church from it.

In all this there is just enough element of truth to make it specious, but insufficient to make it convincing. For, if there is spiritual peril in the retention of the Old Testament, there is vastly more in its rejection. The Old Testament has been the Bible of the Church from its inception, and the New Testament cannot be understood save in relation to the Old. For its roots lie in the Old, and keep it firmly grounded in history. For Christianity is not a body of doctrines and speculations. It is a way of life, and an attitude of soul to God and man, born of an inner experience of spirit. That experience of spirit is new for each one of us, but it comes to us not in an unmediated illumination, but vitally linked to the historical revelation of God in Christ, and beyond that to the historical revelation of God in Israel.

It is, of course, true that to us the Old Testament is a human achievement, but I have sufficiently indicated that it can never be properly understood if it is regarded as a merely human achievement. For God was in human experience, revealing Himself to those who had eyes to behold Him, speaking to those who had ears to hear, and awaking to life the spirits of those who were sensitive to His touch. When they set down their experiences, their visions, their understanding of things spiritual, they were not recording something which they had achieved for themselves, but something which was given them by God, given in the measure of their capacity to receive and their willingness to receive.

It is, of course, true that to us the Old Testament is no longer an infallible text-book of history, though, even from an historical standpoint, it is far more reliable than other ancient documents of comparable antiquity. Our respect for the historical worth of the Old Testament, while, in some respects, more sober than that of our fathers, is no less deep. But he who only goes to the Old Testament for history misses its deepest and richest message. For while, as I have said, the faith of Judaism was rooted and grounded in history, it is far from exhausted in history. It was deeply and vitally interested in history, because it sought to learn the lessons of history, and because it sought to find God in history. And the writers of the Old Testament are more concerned to unfold the lessons of history, and to reveal the God Who had revealed Himself in history, than they are to record the history for its own sake. And he, who would rightly read the Old Testament, must read it not as a mere record of events, but as the vehicle of a great revelation.

It is true, of course, that there is much in the Old Testament of a sub-Christian level. But in common fairness it must be added that there is much that is below the level of Judaism. For the Old Testament covers a long period of development, and sets forth a long process of growth in the understanding of God. Again and again, some great soul, who had entered into the inheritance of his predecessors, received some new revelation through his own experience, transcended the level of those who had gone before, and left a richer inheritance for those who came after.

There is peril in regarding the Old Testament as on a common level of authority and worth, as setting forth in all its parts a view of God and of duty that offers equally the standard for our acceptance. There is peril in being so immersed in the critical and historical study of the Old Testament that it ceases to be for us primarily a collection of religious literature. There is peril in the detached study of the religious growth of Israel from obscure and mean origins through the prophetic struggle to a purer theology. But there is no peril in regarding it as a matchless record of the spiritual experience of men, that can continually speak words relevant to our experience. In its teaching of God and man there is much that is still true for us. But it has something more to give than any specific teaching. It is throughout penetrated by the realization that life has meaning in so far as God is in it, and that God not alone unveils Himself in human experience, but clothes Himself with human personality. His spirit can enter man, and make him His own mouthpiece, the vehicle of His revelation and of His will. Yet, when the spirit of God fills him, he is none the less himself, with his own individuality and outlook.

To understand this literature is worth all the effort it costs, and that understanding is crowned when it leads to a like recognition that God, Who is other than we are, comes to us in our experience, clothes Himself with our personality, makes us the instruments of His will, teaches us in the things that we suffer, delivers us by the greatness of His power. It reveals to us the spirit of man in all its moods ; it ministers to the spirit of man in all its moods.

I am very conscious that in these chapters I have dealt very imperfectly with my subject. It is my hope that I have been fair to Judaism, and have shown something of its relevance to our modern world. The exclusive features of its particularism, so unattractive to us, had yet a part to play, and claim our recognition of debt to them. Still more those noble visions of the universal reign of righteousness and of God, those high conceptions of a world mission, those penetrating glimpses of the springs of spiritual power, and all the rich treasure contained in the life and thought and literature of Israel, have proved an abiding source of blessing to the world, because they have passed beyond Judaism into Christianity. In humble gratitude to Israel and to her God we appropriate the inheritance she bequeathed, remembering with honour the oft nameless seers to whom it was given, and recognizing that with the gift there comes a task. For the mission of Israel to the Gentiles, claimed and appropriated by the Church, is yet incompletely fulfilled.

BOOKS RECOMMENDED FOR FURTHER STUDY

This list makes no pretence to be exhaustive, but merely suggests to the interested reader some of the sources for further study.

A

THE HISTORICAL BACKGROUND

E. R. BEVAN—
The House of Seleucus, 2 vols., 1902, London.
Jerusalem under the High Priest, 1904, London.
A History of Egypt under the Ptolemaic Dynasty, 1927, London.

A. BOUCHÉ-LECLERCQ—
Histoire des Lagides, 4 vols., 1903–7, Paris.
Histoire des Séleucides, 2 vols., 1913–14, Paris.

G. H. BOX, *Judaism in the Greek Period* (*Clarendon Bible*), 1932, Oxford.

Cambridge Ancient History, vols. iv.–x., 1926–34, Cambridge.

R. KITTEL, *Geschichte des Volkes Israel*, iii., 1927–29, Stuttgart.

W. F. LOFTHOUSE, *Israel after the Exile* (*Clarendon Bible*), 1928, Oxford.

W. O. E. OESTERLEY, *History of Israel*, ii., 1932, Oxford.

G. RICCIOTTI, *Storia d'Israele*, ii., 1934, Torino.

H. W. ROBINSON, *The History of Israel : Its Facts and Factors*, 1938, London.

A. SCHLATTER, *Geschichte Israels von Alexander dem Grossen bis Hadrian*, 3rd ed., 1925, Stuttgart.

E. SCHURER, *Geschichte des jüdischen Volkes im Zeitalter Jesu Christi*, 4th ed., 3 vols. and index, 1901–11, Leipzig. (The E.T., published under the title *History of the Jewish People in the Time of Jesus Christ*, 5 vols. and index, 1890, Edinburgh, is made from the second German edition.)

B

THE THOUGHT AND PRACTICE OF JUDAISM

I. ABRAHAMS, *Studies in Pharisaism and the Gospels*, 2 vols., 1917–24, Cambridge.

W. H. BENNETT, *The Religion of the Post-Exilic Prophets*, 1907, Edinburgh.

E. R. BEVAN and C. SINGER (ed. by), *The Legacy of Israel*, 1927, Oxford.

J. BONSIRVEN, *Le Judaïsme Palestinien*, 2 vols., 1934, Paris.

W. BOUSSET, *Die Religion des Judentums im späthellenistischen Zeitalter*, 1926, Tübingen.

L. E. BROWNE, *Early Judaism*, 1920, Cambridge.

A. CAUSSE—
Israël et la Vision de l'Humanité, 1924, Strasbourg.
Les Dispersés d'Israël, 1929, Strasbourg.
Du Groupe ethnique à la Communauté religieuse, 1938, Strasbourg.

A. DUFF, *A History of the Religion of Judaism*, 500–200 B.C., n.d., London.

C. GUIGNEBERT, *Le Monde Juif vers le temps de Jésus*, 1935, Paris (E.T. by S. H. Hooke, 1938, London).

M.-J. LAGRANGE, *Le Judaïsme avant Jésus-Christ*, 1931, Paris.

A. LODS, *Les Prophètes d'Israël et les débuts du Judaisme*, 1935, Paris (E.T. by S. H. Hooke, 1937, London).

H. LOEWE (ed. by), *The Contact of Pharisaism with other Cultures*, 1937, London.

G. F. MOORE, *Judaism in the First Centuries of the Christian Era*, 3 vols., 1927–30, Cambridge, Mass.

W. O. E. OESTERLEY (ed. by), *The Age of Transition*, 1937, London.

A. S. PEAKE (ed. by), *The People and the Book*, 1925, Oxford.

H. W. ROBINSON (ed. by), *Record and Revelation*, 1938, Oxford.

C

THE SERVANT SONGS

In addition to treatment in the Commentaries noted below.

C. BUDDE, *Die sogenannten Ebed-Jahwe-Lieder und die Bedeutung des Knechtes Jahwes in Jes. 40–55*, 1900, Giessen.

O. EISSFELDT, *The Ebed-Jahwe in Isaiah xl.–lv. in the Light of the Israelite Conceptions of the Community and the Individual, the Ideal and the Real*, (*Expository Times*, xliv., pp. 261–8), 1933, Edinburgh.

J. FISCHER—

    Isaias 40–55 und die Perikopen vom Gottesknecht (*Alttestamentliche Abhandlungen*, VI. 4–5), 1916, Münster i. W.

    Wer ist der Ebed in den Perikopen Js. 42, 1–7 ; 49, 1–9a ; 50, 4–9 ; 52, 13–53, 12 ? (*Alttest. Abhand.* VIII. 5), 1922, Münster i. W.

H. GRESSMANN, *Der Messias*, 1929, Göttingen (pp. 287–339).

R. H. KENNETT, *The ' Servant of the Lord,'* 1911, London.

S. MOWINCKEL, *Der Knecht Jahwäs*, 1921, Giessen.

A. S. PEAKE, *The Servant of Yahweh*, 1931, Manchester.

J. S. VAN DER PLOEG, *Les Chants du Serviteur de Jahvé dans la seconde partie du Livre d'Isaïe*, 1936, Paris.

H. W. ROBINSON—

    The Cross of the Servant, 1926, London.

    The Hebrew Conception of Corporate Personality (in *Werden und Wesen des Alten Testaments*, ed. J. Hempel, pp. 49–62), 1936, Berlin.

W. RUDOLPH, *Der exilische Messias* (*Zeitschrift für die alt-testamentliche Wissenschaft*, xli., pp. 90–114), 1925, Giessen.

E. SELLIN—

Tritojesaja, Deuterojesaja und das Gottesknechtsproblem (*Nene Kirkliche Zeitschrift*, xli., pp. 73–93, 145–173), 1930, Leipzig.

Die Lösung des deuterojesajanischen Gottesknechtsrätsels, (ZAW lv., pp. 177–217), 1937, Giessen.

W. STAERK, *Die Ebed Jahwe-Lieder in Jesaja 40 ff.* (*Beiträge zur Wissenschaft vom Alten Testament*, xiv.), 1913, Leipzig.

D

COMMENTARIES

(a) DEUTERO- AND TRITO-ISAIAH

G. H. BOX, *The Book of Isaiah*, 1916, London.

K. BUDDE, *Das Buch Jesaia Kap.* 40–66 (Kautzsch-Bertholet, *Die Heilige Schrift des Alten Testaments*, i., pp. 653–720), 1922, Tübingen.

A. CONDAMIN, *Le Livre d'Isaïe* (*Études Bibliques*), 1905, Paris.

B. DUHM, *Das Buch Jesaia* (Nowack, *Handkommentar zum Alten Testament*, III. i.), 1892, Göttingen.

F. FELDMANN, *Das Buch Isaias* (Nikel and Schulz, *Exegetisches Handbuch zum Alten Testament*, XIV. ii.), 1926, Münster i. W.

L. KÖHLER, *Deuterojesaja stilkritisch untersucht* (*BZAW* 37), 1923, Giessen.

E. KÖNIG, *Das Buch Jesaja*, 1926, Gütersloh.

R. LEVY, *Deutero-Isaiah*, 1925, Oxford.

K. MARTI, *Das Buch Jesaja* (Marti, *Kurzer Hand-Commentar zum Alten Testament* X.), 1900, Tübingen.

J. SKINNER, *The Book of the Prophet Isaiah, Chapters xl.–lxvi.* (*Cambridge Bible*), 1917, Cambridge.

C. C. TORREY, *The Second Isaiah*, 1928, Edinburgh.

P. VOLZ, *Jesaia II.* (Sellin's *Kommentar zum Alten Testament* IX.), 1932, Leipzig.

G. W. Wade, *The Book of the Prophet Isaiah* (*Westminster Commentaries*), 1911, London.

O. C. Whitehouse, *Isaiah xl.–lxvi.* (*Century Bible*), n.d., London.

(b) Malachi

A. von Bulmerincq, *Der Prophet Maleachi*, 2 vols., 1926–32, Dorpat (Tartu).

C. Lattey, *The Book of Malachi* (*Westminster Version of the Sacred Scriptures*), 1934, London.

K. Marti, *Das Dodekapropheten* (Marti, *KHC* XIII.), 1904, Tübingen.

W. Nowack, *Die Kleinen Propheten* (Nowack, *HK* III. iv.), 1897, Göttingen.

E. Sellin, *Das Zwölfprophetenbuch* (Sellin, *KAT* XII.), 1929–1930, Leipzig.

J. M. P. Smith, *A Critical and Exegetical Commentary on the book of Malachi* (*International Critical Commentary*), 1912, Edinburgh.

(c) Jonah (see also under Malachi).

J. A. Bewer, *A Critical and Exegetical Commentary on the book of Jonah* (*ICC*), 1912, Edinburgh.

T. E. Bird, *The Book of Jonah* (*WVSS*), 1938, London.

G. W. Wade, *The Books of the Prophets Micah, Obadiah, Joel, and Jonah* (*WC*), 1925, London.

(d) Ruth

G. A. Cooke, *The Books of Judges and Ruth* (*Cambridge Bible*), 1918, Cambridge.

P. Joüon, *Ruth: Commentaire philologique et exégétique*, 1924, Rome.

C. Lattey, *The Book of Ruth* (*WVSS*), 1935, London.

INDEX

(a) GENERAL

Abrahams, I., 103.
Ahab, 109.
Alexander the Great, 51.
Antiochus Epiphanes, 52, 54 ff.
Baptism, 62, 103 f.
Bonsirven, J., 63.
Burkitt, F. C., 103.
Chasidhim, 58.
Circumcision, 62, 102.
Confucius, 106 f.
Daniel, 64, 82, 115 f.
David, 46 f., 81, 108.
Deutero-Isaiah, 7 ff., 26, 28, 33, 42, 44, 49, 71.
Deuteronomy, 41, 110.
Deutero-Zechariah, 37.
Elijah, 40, 108.
Enoch, 66.
2 Esdras, *see* 4 Ezra.
Ethical religion of Israel, 104 ff.
Ezra, 42, 45 ff., 51.
4 Ezra, 68 ff.
' God-fearers,' 62, 74.
Gray, G. B., 4.
Habakkuk, 4 f.
Haggai, 43.
Herodians, 75.
Hillel, 63.
History as vehicle of revelation, 111 ff.
Hosea, 33, 114, 118.
Hu Shih, 111.
Isaiah, 2 f.
Islam, 112.
Jehoiachin, 11.
Jeremiah, 6 f., 11, 41, 102 f., 114 f., 124.
Jerome, 55.
Job, 115.

Joel, 92.
Jonah, 32 ff., 44, 89, 118.
Jose ben Kisma, 73.
Josephus, 63.
Joüon, P., 36 n.
Loewe, H., 63.
Lord's Supper, 103 f.
Malachi, 29 f., 45, 63.
Manson, T. W., 66 n., 82 n.
Marti, K., 21 n.
Mencius, 106.
Messel, N., 66 n.
Messianic Prophecy, 5, 11, 13, 64 ff., 81 ff., 93.
Micah, 2 f.
Monotheism and its corollary, 7 ff.
Montefiore, C. G., 68 n.
Moore, G. F., 62.
Moses, 11, 103 f., 107 f., 112.
Nehemiah, 42, 45 ff.
Oesterley, W. O. E., 68.
Paul, 31, 88.
Peter, 92.
Pharisees and Pharisaism, 58 f., 75 ff., 86.
Philo, 63.
Prophecy, Fulfilment of, 89 ff.
Proselytes, 28, 47 f., 50, 59, 62 f., 101.
Psalter, 35 ff., 121 f.
Resurrection, 115 f.
Robinson, H. W., 11.
Ruth, 46 ff.
Sadducees, 58, 75.
Sellin, E., 84.
Servant of Yahweh, 10 ff., 83 ff., 89, 100.
Servant Songs, 10 ff., 85, 89, 94.
Sibylline Oracles, 67.

(*b*) Texts